Sushi Chef
Sukiyabashi Jiro

Shinzo Satomi

Photography by Yohei Maruyama

Translated by Rei Perovic

VERTICAL.

Table of Contents

Chapter 3
Prepping the Four Seasons' Nigiri-159

Work of Sukiyabashi Jiro:
Follow His Preparation Process-177

Chapter 4
Nori Maki, Tamagoyaki-206

Jiro Sushi Talk 4
Nori Maki, Tamagoyaki-207

Chapter 5
Of Sumeshi-233

Jiro Sushi Talk 5
Of Sumeshi-243

Idle Talk Between a Sushi Restaurant Pops and His Regular-254

PREFACE
INVITATION TO JIRO ONO'S WORLD

This book is the ultimate "*Edomae* (Tokyo Bay)-style Nigiri Sushi Technical Manual," and without omission includes all of the nigiri, sake sides, and small dishes served over the course of the year by the number-one sushi craftsman of the present day, Jiro Ono.

When you peek into a plain wood *tane* box that's unique to the Sukiyabashi Jiro establishment, it's clear which seafood is in season in the oceans around Japan. The king of whitefish in the cold season is *hirame* (flounder), while *fukko* (young Japanese sea bass) and *mako garei* (marbled sole) reign in summer. Octopus tentacles become flavorful in winter, *awabi* (abalone) is in season in the Kanto area in summer. *Shako* (mantis shrimp) can be found in the market all year round, but they taste the best when they're in the spawning phase in the springtime. In short, this book is highly useful as "a glossary of seasonal seafood."

Moreover, he didn't simply demonstrate his brilliant and delicate technique. He also exhaustively disclosed the secrets to the flavors of his renowned restaurant.

Hon maguro (bluefin tuna) marinated in soy sauce. Pickled *kohada* (gizzard shad). Steamed *awabi* (abalone). Simmered *anago* (conger eel). Boiled *tako* (octopus). Boiled *kuruma ebi* (prawn). Marinated *hamaguri* (hard clam). Marinated *shako* (mantis shrimp). Minced *shiba ebi* (shiba shrimp). *Tamagoyaki* (Japanese omelette). Furthermore, how to cook vinegared rice. To smoke *katsuo* (bonito). A tip to keeping the freshness of *katsuo* until nighttime. A reasonable thawing method for *ikura* (salmon roe). Selection techniques for *kanpyo* (dried gourd). The way to toast *nori* (dried seaweed) and the seasoning of *gari* (pickled ginger). Needless to say, these are secret formulae that have never been taken out of the sushi restaurants. Here lies the reason we call it "the ultimate."

The nigiri that Jiro Ono makes is noble and beautiful. *Kohada's* liveliness, expressed by twisting the tip of the tail a tad to the left. Steamed *awabi* (abalone) ever so soft that hugs the vinegared rice marvelously. *Iwashi* (sardine) that shows the freshness of the catch through the dark flesh. Aromatic *hatsu gatsuo* (the first bonito of the season) smoked with straw fire. The appetite-stimulating refined fat of marbled *kinkai hon maguro* (bluefin tuna from the seas around Japan) and bellows belly of *otoro* (fatty tuna). Brilliantly colored and aromatic *nori maki* (vinegared rice rolled in seaweed) with its *nori* toasted with *Kishu bincho* charcoal every morning. Readers are in for a visual feast every time they turn a page.

Take *maguro* (tuna) for example. When you look at the pictures of the whole fish cut in round slices, you can clearly see the exact locations of lean meat, the *chutoro* (medium-fatty tuna), the bellows belly of *otoro* (fatty tuna), and marbling at a glance. I pat myself on the back that this book is a valuable record that's very useful for sushi craftsmen and enthusiasts, not to mention market participants. To cut an expensive *kinkai hon maguro* into round slices is unprecedented.

In the beginning, I wrote, "the number-one sushi craftsman of the present day, Jiro Ono." This statement is certainly not an exaggeration. He not only possesses the outstanding sense of smell, sense of taste, and taste-bud memory required to be a first-class chef, but is also an extraordinarily tenacious perfectionist and obsessive.

Ono works relentlessly to improve the flavors. And the nigiri he makes evolves on a daily basis. For instance, he used to boil *kuruma ebi* (prawn) twice a day, in the morning and at night, but now he cooks it right after taking the order and makes lukewarm nigiri. And he now sticks to only the wild ones from Tokyo Bay. He knows from trial and error that "*kuruma ebi's* natural flavor is exerted at its aromatic best at body temperature." And "after boiling, the red and white of the wild prawn from Tokyo Bay is the most beautiful compared to other places." It's not just *kuruma ebi*. Every technique performed on each *tane* (topping) advances rapidly. Therefore, each time I visit, I discover a "new heavenly body" that is bliss in my mouth.

Where does his persistent spirit of inquiry come from?

When young Ono was a cook in Hamamatsu, he aspired to be a sushi chef and at the age of twenty-six, in spring, entered an apprenticeship at the prestigious *Edomae*-style nigiri restaurant Yoshino (in Kyobashi, Tokyo). It was a late restart. He diligently learned by observing and imitating the techniques of his predecessor at Yoshino, Suekichi Yoshino (deceased), who was famed as a maestro. The way Ono toasts *nori* and creates the flavor of *anago* originated from what he learned back then and developed according to his own style. Three years later, Jiro was ordered to go to Osaka to head a restaurant for hire, and there, he encountered authentic *tako* (octopus) from Akashi. Ono started to display his perfectionism after he returned to Tokyo at the age of thirty-three. Using the local octopus of Kanto, he attempted through trial and error to recreate the flavor and aroma of octopus from Akashi. And at last, he determined that "the natural octopus flavor is exerted at its aromatic best at body temperature" and that "for the accompanying flavor, it is better to use coarse salt instead of the traditional sweet and salty *Edomae*-style *nitsume* (reduction sauce)."

- I don't make nigiri with *tai* (sea bream)
- Expensive and rare *hoshi garei* (starry flounder) is not the king of whitefish
- It's out of pride as a sushi craftsman that I disregard profit and make *shinko* (young gizzard shad) nigiri
- Without vinegared rice at body temperature, you can't make tasty nigiri
- There is no particular order to eat nigiri
- Immediately after I make the nigiri, put it in your mouth

Reading the "Jiro Sushi Talk" in this book feels like listening to a maestro talk about his art.

It's been a half-century since a young man with great ambitions came to the Eastern capital during the chaotic era of the ruin-of-fire black market. Jiro Ono, who was born in 1925, managed to establish a famous *Edomae*-style nigiri sushi restaurant in his lifetime. To this day, he, long past the age of seventy, still stands in his kitchen and makes nigiri. And he continues to watch over how much vinegar his young apprentices use for *kohada* and the seasoning condition of the vinegared rice. His painstaking pursuit to improve his sushi *tane* continues.

Chapter 1

Nigiri-*dane* in Spring and Summer

Surprisingly cozy, ten counter seats and thirteen table seats. When the guests arrive, Jiro out of plain wood from the back and puts them down on the room-temperature *tsuke dai*

The restaurant is located in the basement of a building close to the Tokyo Metro Marunouchi Line Ginza Station.

carries *tane bako* ingredient boxes made counter.

When you enter through the sliding door, there is a hanging lantern and washbasin made out of Izu stone.

*The locations of the catch and landing were noted as the areas of origin of the fish. However, if the origins were noted as Hokkaido, Kyushu, etc., at the market, then we conformed to them.

<SPRING> DISH

From bottom row left:
Tori Gai/cockles (Atsumi)
Shako/mantis shrimp (Koshiba)
Anago/conger eel (Nojima)
Tamagoyaki/Japanese omelette (Okukuji)

Second row:
Aka Gai/surf clam (Yuriage)
Kohada/gizzard shad (Saga)
Kuruma Ebi/prawn (Yokosuka)
Aji/horse mackerel (Futtsu)

Making Spring Nigiri

Third row:
Chutoro/medium-fatty tuna (Noborito)
Fukko/young sea bass (Joban)
Aori Ika/bigfin reef squid (Kyushu)

Fourth row:
Tekka Maki/tuna roll (Noborito)

Plate: Hagi Yaki

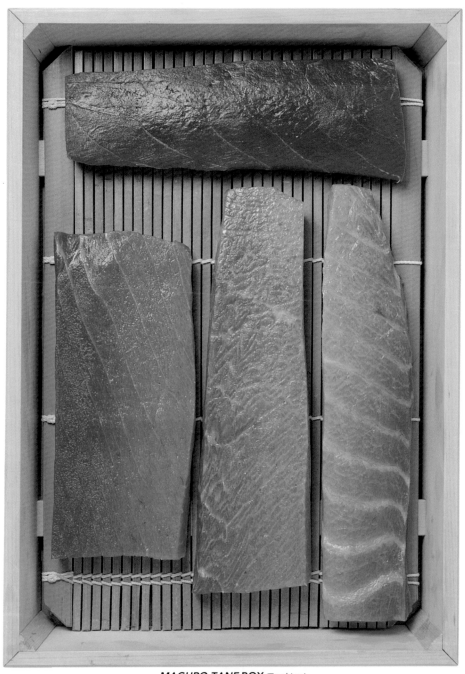

***MAGURO TANE* BOX** (Tsushima)
From bottom row left: ***Chutoro*/medium-fatty tuna**, ***Otoro*/fatty tuna** (marbled), ***Otoro*/fatty tuna** (bellows belly)
Top: **Lean Meat**

<SPRING> BOX ONE
From the bottom: *Katsuo*/bonito (Boshu Katsuura), *Iwashi*/sardine (Nagai), *Aji*/horse mackerel (Futtsu), *Shako*/mantis shrimp (Koshiba), *Kohada*/gizzard shad (Kyushu), *Kuruma Ebi*/prawn (Tokyo Bay)

15

<SPRING> BOX TWO
Bottom: *Inada/*young yellowtail (Misaki) From top left: *Aori Ika/*bigfin reef squid (Nagasaki),
*Mako Garei/*marbled sole (Joban), *Fukko/*young Japanese sea bass (Joban)

16

<SPRING> BOX THREE
From bottom row left: *Aka Gai*/surf clam (Yuriage), *Aka Gai no Himo*/string of surf clam (Yuriage)
Second row: *Nama Awabi*/raw abalone (Iwawada), *Tori Gai*/cockles (Ise)
Third row: *Kobashira*/small scallops (Hokkaido), *Miru Gai*/geoduck clam (Atsumi)

17

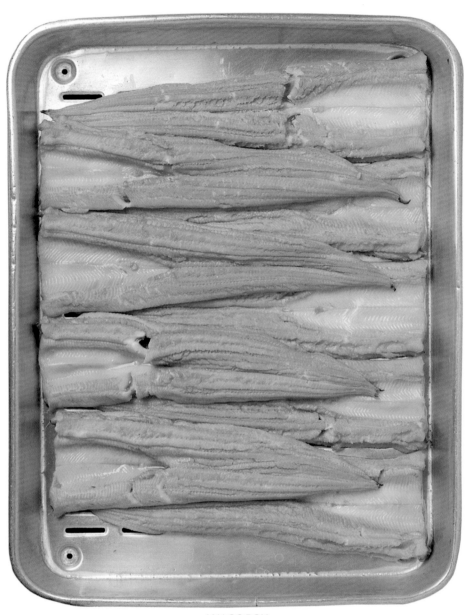

***ANAGO* BOX**
(Nojima, Tokyo Bay)

From left: *Kohada*/gizzard shad (Kyushu), *Aori Ika*/bigfin reef squid (Nagasaki),
Chutoro/medium-fatty tuna (Sanriku)

From left: *Kohada*/gizzard shad (Kyushu), *Aka Gai*/surf clam (Yuriage), *Aori Ika*/bigfin reef squid (Nagasaki)

From left: *Chutoro*/medium-fatty tuna (Sanriku), *Mako Garei*/marbled sole (Joban)

(raw hors d'oeuvre)
<SPRING> *NAMA TSUMAMI:* THREE KINDS

(sake side dish)
<SPRING> *SHUKOU* : broad beans
When you order sake,
seasonal "greens" are served.

19

<SUMMER> DISH

From bottom row left: *Suzuki*/Japanese sea bass (Joban), *Anago*/conger eel (Nojima), *Tamagoyaki*/Japanese omelette (Okukuji)
Second row: *Shima Aji*/striped jack (Boshu Katsuyama), *Kuruma Ebi*/prawn (Tokyo Bay), *Nama Awabi*/raw abalone (Iwawada), *Koika*/small squid (Izumi), *Mako Garei*/marbled sole (Joban)

20

Making Summer Nigiri

Third row: *Kyuri Maki*/cucumber roll, *Aka Gai*/surf clam (Ise), *Shinko*/young gizzard shad (Ariake Sea)

<SUMMER> BOX ONE
From bottom left: *Koika no Geso/*small squid tentacles (Izumi), *Kuruma Ebi/*prawn (Tokyo Bay)
From top left: *Iwashi/*sardine (Choshi), *Shinko/*young gizzard shad, *maruzuke* (one per nigiri) and
nimaizuke (two per nigiri) sizes (Ariake Sea), *Aji/*horse mackerel (Futtsu,Tokyo Bay)

<SUMMER> BOX TWO
Bottom: *Koika*/small squid (Izumi) From top left: *Suzuki*/sea bass (Joban),
Mako Garei/marbled sole (Joban), *Shima Aji*/striped jack (Boshu Katusyama)

<SUMMER> BOX THREE
Bottom: *Uni/*sea urchin (Hokkaido)
Second row: *Nama Awabi/*raw abalone (Iwawada), *Kobashira/*small scallops (Hokkaido)
Third row: *Aka Gai/*surf clam (Kyushu), *Aka Gai no Himo/*string of surf clam (Kyushu)

Mushi Awabi/steamed abalone
(Iwawada)

(sake side dish)
<SUMMER> *SHUKOU* : Edamame

<SUMMER> *NAMA TSUMAMI* (raw hors d'oeuvre)
From the front: *Shinko*/young gizzard shad (Ariake Sea), *Koika*/small squid (Kyushu)
Back: *Shima Aji*/striped jack (Boshu Katusyama)

Tane boxes arranged on the counter

Tesu (hand-dipping vinegar), *sabi choko* (small wasabi bowl), *nitsuke* (reduction sauce), *nikiri* (thin and sweet glaze)

Tsuma Ire (containers for sushi accompaniments): *shoga* (ginger), wasabi, *kyuri* (cucumber), *myoga* (Japanese ginger), *oba* (perilla), etc.

Flowers from the field which decorate the entrance from March to September. One can feel nature's seasons from the flowers, too.

Gui nomi (sake cups) made by artists line up on the display shelf next to the counter.

27

<AUTUMN> DISH

From bottom row left:
*Anago/*conger eel (Nojima)
*Hamaguri/*hard clam (Ise)
*Tamagoyaki/*Japanese omelette (Okukuji)

Second row:
*Saba/*mackerel (Fukuoka)
*Kohada/*gizzard shad (Atsumi)
*Sayori/*halfbeak (Futtsu)
*Aka Gai/*surf clam (Yuriage)

Making Autumn Nigiri

Third row:
Soge/young flounder (Joban)
Otoro/fatty tuna (Oma)
Shokko/young greater amberjack (Boshu)

Back row:
Oboro Maki

Plate: Tenryu Yaki

<AUTUMN> BOX ONE
From the bottom: *Kuruma Ebi*/prawn (Futtsu), *Sayori*/halfbeak (Futtsu)
From top left: *Kohada*/gizzard shad (Yamaguchi), *Iwashi*/sardine (Futtsu), *Saba*/mackerel (Fukuoka)

<AUTUMN> BOX TWO
From the bottom: *Tako*/octopus (Sajima), *Sumi Ika*/squid (Ise), *Shokko*/young greater amberjack (Boshu),
Engawa (little flesh on the fin) of *Soge*/young flounder (Aomori), *Soge*/young flounder (Aomori)

31

<AUTUMN> BOX THREE
From the bottom left: *Aka Gai/*surf clam (Yuriage), *Aka Gai no Himo/*string of surf clam (Yuriage)
Second row: *Miru Gai/*geoduck clam (Atsumi), *Hamaguri/*hard clam (Ise)
Third row: *Kobashira/*small scallops (Hokkaido), *Nama Ikura/*raw salmon roe (Sanriku)

In October, the restaurant is redecorated. The lighting becomes slightly brighter. When you make a reservation, they assign your seat, set chopsticks on the counter, and pull out the chair a little.

(raw hors d'oeuvre)
<AUTUMN> *NAMA TSUMAMI*

From left: ***Tako/*octopus** (Sajima), ***Saba/*mackerel** (Fukuoka), ***Shokko/*young greater amberjack** (Boshu)

(sake side dish)
<AUTUMN> *SHUKOU*

At the beginning of autumn comes *ao ginnan* (green ginkgo nuts), and eventually you see yellow *ginnan*.

33

<WINTER> DISH

From bottom row left: *Aka Gai/*surf clam (Yuriage), *Anago/*conger eel (Nojima), *Uni/*sea urchin (Hokkaido), *Tamagoyaki/*Japanese omelette (Okukuji)
Second row: *Kohada/*gizzard shad (Kyushu), *Sumi Ika/*squid (Nagasaki), *Inada/*young yellowtail (Tateyama), *Saba/*mackerel (Choshi)

Making Winter Nigiri

Third row:
Otoro/fatty tuna (Sado), *Akami*/tuna lean meat (Sado), *Hirame*/flounder (Aomori)
Back row:
Kanpyo Maki/dried gourd roll

Plate: Tenryu Yaki

<WINTER> BOX ONE
From the bottom: *Kuruma Ebi/*prawn (Futtsu), *Sayori/*halfbeak (Oarai)
From top left: *Kohada/*gizzard shad, *maruzuke* (one per nigiri) and *katamizuke*
(one side per nigiri) sizes (Saga), *Saba/*mackerel (Choshi)

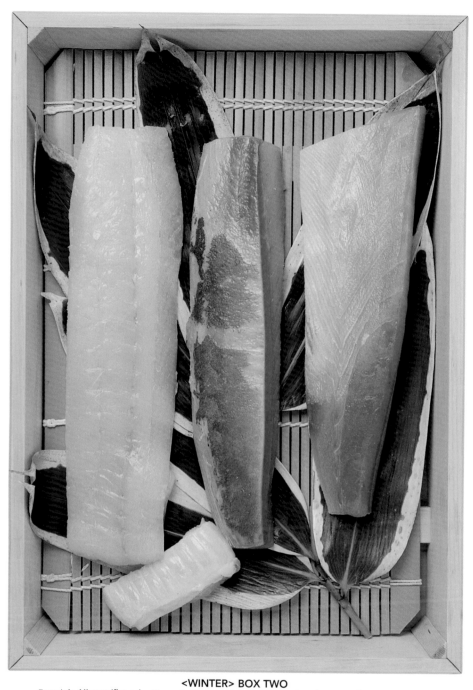

\<WINTER\> BOX TWO
From left: *Hirame*/flounder (Aomori), *Engawa* (little flesh on the fin) of *Hirame*/flounder (Aomori),
Back and belly of *Inada*/young yellowtail (Tateyama)

<WINTER> BOX THREE
From the bottom: *Tako*/octopus (Sajima), *Nama Ikura*/raw salmon roe (Sanriku),
Uni/sea urchin (Hokkaido), *Hamaguri*/hard clam (Ise)

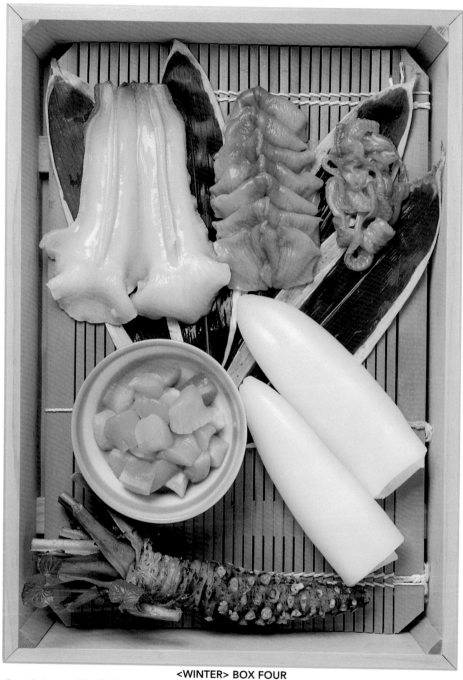

<WINTER> BOX FOUR

From the bottom: **Wasabi** (three years old, Tenjo), **Kobashira/small scallops** (Hokkaido), **Sumi Ika/squid** (Choshi)
From top left: **Miru Gai/geoduck clam** (Atsumi), **Aka Gai/surf clam** (Yuriage),
Aka Gai no Himo/string of surf clam (Yuriage)

39

(raw hors d'oeurve) (sake side dish)
<WINTER> *NAMA TSUMAMI* AND *SHUKOU*
From the left: *Aka Gai/*surf clam (Yuriage), *Aka Gai no Himo/*string of surf clam (Yuriage), *Inada/*young yellowtail (Tateyama), *Sayori/*halfbeak (Oarai)

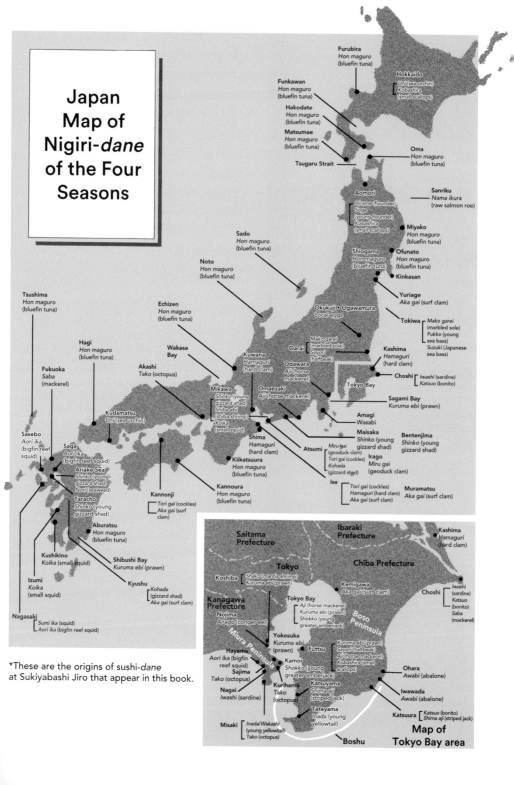

Japan Map of Nigiri-*dane* of the Four Seasons

Furubira
Hon maguro
(bluefin tuna)

Hokkaido
Uni (sea urchin)
Kobashira
(small scallops)

Funkawan
Hon maguro
(bluefin tuna)

Hakodate
Hon maguro
(bluefin tuna)

Matsumae
Hon maguro
(bluefin tuna)

Oma
Hon maguro
(bluefin tuna)

Tsugaru Strait

Sanriku
Nama ikura
(raw salmon roe)

Aomori
Hirame (flounder)
Sogo
(young flounder)
Kobashira
(small scallops)

Miyako
Hon maguro
(bluefin tuna)

Sado
Hon maguro
(bluefin tuna)

Shiogama
Hon maguro
(bluefin tuna)

Ofunato
Hon maguro
(bluefin tuna)

Kinkasan

Noto
Hon maguro
(bluefin tuna)

Yuriage
Aka gai (surf clam)

Tsushima
Hon maguro
(bluefin tuna)

Echizen
Hon maguro
(bluefin tuna)

Okukuji • Ogawamura
Local eggs

Tokiwa
Mako garei
(marbled sole)
Fukko (young
sea bass)
Suzuki (Japanese
sea bass)

Hagi
Hon maguro
(bluefin tuna)

Wakasa
Bay

Oarai
Mako garei
(marbled sole)
Sayori
(halfbeak)

Kashima
Hamaguri (hard clam)

Fukuoka
Saba
(mackerel)

Akashi
Tako (octopus)

Kuwana
Hamaguri
(hard clam)

Odawara
Aji (horse
mackerel)

Choshi
Iwashi (sardine)
Katsuo (bonito)

Tokyo Bay

Kudamatsu
Uni (sea urchin)

Mikawa
Shinko (young
gizzard shad)
Shiba ebi
(shiba shrimp)
Koika
(small squid)

Omaezaki
Aji (horse mackerel)

Sagami Bay
Kuruma ebi (prawn)

Sasebo
Aori ika
(bigfin reef
squid)

Saga
Aori ika
(bigfin reef squid)

Ariake Sea
Shinko (young
gizzard shad)
Nori (seaweed)

Shima
Hamaguri
(hard clam)

Atsumi

Amagi
Wasabi

Maisaka
Shinko (young
gizzard shad)

Bentenjima
Shinko (young
gizzard shad)

Miru gai
(geoduck clam)
Tori gai (cockles)
Kohada
(gizzard shad)

Irago
Miru gai
(geoduck clam)

Taracho
Shinko (young
gizzard shad)

Kiikatsuura
Hon maguro
(bluefin tuna)

Kannonji
Tori gai (cockles)
Aka gai (surf
clam)

Kannoura
Hon maguro
(bluefin tuna)

Ise
Tori gai (cockles)
Hamaguri (hard clam)
Aka gai (surf clam)

Muramatsu
Aka gai (surf clam)

Aburatsu
Hon maguro
(bluefin tuna)

Kushikino
Koika (small squid)

Shibushi Bay
Kuruma ebi (prawn)

Izumi
Koika
(small squid)

Kyushu

Kohada
(gizzard shad)
Aka gai (surf clam)

Nagasaki
Sumi ika (squid)
Aori ika (bigfin reef squid)

*These are the origins of sushi-*dane*
at Sukiyabashi Jiro that appear in this book.

Map of Tokyo Bay area

Saitama
Prefecture

Ibaraki
Prefecture

Kashima
Hamaguri
(hard clam)

Tokyo

Chiba Prefecture

Koshiba
Shako (mantis shrimp)
Kuruma ebi (prawn)

Kemigawa
Aka gai (surf clam)

Choshi
Iwashi
(sardine)
Katsuo
(bonito)
Saba
(mackerel)

Kanagawa
Prefecture

Nojima
Anago (conger eel)

Tokyo Bay
Aji (horse mackerel)
Kuruma ebi (prawn)
Shokko (young
greater amberjack)

Boso
Peninsula

Yokosuka
Kuruma ebi
(prawn)

Futtsu
Kuruma ebi (prawn)
Sayori (halfbeak)
Aji (horse mackerel)
Kobashira (small
scallops)

Miura Peninsula

Hayama
Aori ika (bigfin
reef squid)

Kamoi
Shokko (young
greater amberjack)

Ohara
Awabi (abalone)

Sajima
Tako (octopus)

Kurihama
Tako
(octopus)

Katsuyama
Shima aji
(striped jack)

Iwawada
Awabi (abalone)

Nagai
Iwashi (sardine)

Katsuura
Katsuo (bonito)
Shima aji (striped jack)

Tateyama
Inada (young
yellowtail)

Misaki
Inada/Wakashi
(young yellowtail)
Tako (octopus)

Boshu

NIGIRI-*DANE* IN SPRING AND SUMMER

Seafood in this chapter
Kohada (gizzard shad), *Shinko* (young gizzard shad), *Iwashi* (sardine), *Aji* (horse mackerel), *Mako Garei* (marbled sole), *Fukko* (young sea bass), *Suzuki* (Japanese sea bass), *Shima Aji* (striped jack), *Inada* (young yellowtail), *Koika* (small squid), *Aori Ika* (bigfin reef squid), *Tori Gai* (cockles), *Awabi* (abalone), *Anago* (conger eel), *Shako* (mantis shrimp), *Katsuo* (bonito)

"The tastes of first bonito and returning bonito are as different as fresh greenery and autumn foliage, cherry blossoms and chrysanthemums. So I don't make nigiri with it in autumn."

When the plum flowers begin to blossom here and there, the *tane* box at the sushi restaurant is spring at its height. Not long after the *tori gai*'s flesh gets thick and soft, long-awaited *hatsu gatsuo* (the first bonito of the season) come on stage. *Shako, aji, mako garei* and *awabi* season is near. And when *shinko* and *koika* start to appear, it's high summer. In these months, how is Sukiyabashi Jiro master Jiro Ono making nigiri with seafood in season?

Silver-Skinned Fish: *Kohada, Shinko*
"*Yokozuna* of Nigiri" that Makes My Throat Squeak

Kohada (gizzard shad) is the "*Yokozuna* (sumo wrestling champion) of Nigiri." My throat squeaks when I eat it. Everyone laughs at me when I say this, but when I chew on *kohada* nigiri and swallow it, my throat really squeaks. Especially when the *kohada* on top and the sushi rice at the bottom are perfectly in sync.

And that feeling of "Oh...so good!" really starts to sink in.

Of course I think our other nigiri are delicious too. But I just don't get the same level of feeling because my throat's never squeaked while eating other nigiri. *Kohada* is the cheapest fish among all *sushi neta* (sushi ingredients, typically fish), but if you prep it well, it turns into the "*Yokozuna* of Nigiri" that makes my throat squeak.

To prep it well, I examine the nature of the *kohada* thoroughly, then determine how much salt and vinegar I should use. Especially in the case of *shinko* (young gizzard shad), every second matters while prepping. There are differences in fat content, thickness, and the fish's size. If you put them all together and soak them for the same amount of time, I guarantee that we won't be making throat-squeaking nigiri. Precisely because *shinko* is so small, we prep to make it all taste exactly the same by catering to the individual fish, each slightly different in size and form, soaking it in vinegar even a couple of seconds shorter or longer.

I repeatedly tell my apprentices how important this is. Up to this point in the process, you can achieve good results with effort alone.

If my apprentices don't make the fish taste consistent, and if we're not satisfied ourselves, then I'm in trouble as the one who makes the nigiri. Because beyond that, it's inside the guest's mouth, and there's nothing left that I can do.

Speaking of which, when I was traveling in Kyushu, I tried *kohada* nigiri at a sushi restaurant. It smelled fishy; the *kohada* was not pickled well, and it just tasted really bad. My friend and I were whispering, "How did they manage to make this nigiri taste so messed up?" The sushi master mistook our murmurs for compliments and proceeded to proudly explain his prepping process: "I seasoned it with salt for this many minutes and pickled it with vinegar for that many minutes."

The sushi master must not have tried it himself. Clearly, because he hadn't fine-tuned the flavor to a satisfactory level through tasting, the *kohada* nigiri turned into something foul. You don't have to prep them yourself. You can have your apprentices prep them. But you must taste it yourself after the prep. If it starts to taste strange, then you have to tweak it.

It's a big mistake to say, "I'm absolutely certain about what I'm doing."

It's true with everything. Over the years, a small gap, as tiny as the tip of your nail at the outset, ends up as a gaping one.

It works if you create the taste you like and say, "This is it!" and then, "Here you go!" But you're making a mistake if you mindlessly keep serving something that tastes strange and say, "I'm not making a mistake. It's just that our customers have poor taste buds." I keep telling this to my apprentices over and over.

Something like this happened this morning. It seemed like the *shinko* wasn't pickled quite enough. I confirmed it after tasting it. So I told my apprentice, "Sprinkle more salt," because the balance was off with the sushi rice. And I just wasn't satisfied after many adjustments. I kept telling them to try "one more time, one more time," and we ended up running out of it for the lunch service. This sort of thing happens often.

People often tell me, "Why do you keep eating so much *shinko* that's so expensive in season?" I think it would be rude to the guest if I weren't able to say, "This is good!" after tasting it, confident in its quality. We don't make nigiri for free. We charge our guests.

This is why I taste our *neta* repeatedly throughout the day.

Especially with *kohada*, I taste it in the morning, at noon, and in the evening. Then to see how it'll be pickled the next day, I try it again after I close. If I keep tasting it until I'm satisfied, then our customers will never say, "It tastes bad."

However, if I'm feeling a little hungry, I prefer to quickly make nigiri with our *kohada*, which is far more delicious that way. If a guest orders it just to pick on it while drinking sake, I can't help but mumble, "*Kohada* is better as nigiri." Raw seafood like *maguro* (tuna), *ika* (squid), *aka gai* (surf clam), and whitefish don't taste all that different as nigiri or sashimi. But for our *kohada*, we prep it to balance well with our sushi rice, so it's definitely best to have it as nigiri.

It's not only about the balance with sushi rice; we also account for the flavor of the *nikiri shoyu** that we brush onto the *kohada* right before serving. When I eat our prepped *kohada* with our sushi rice and *nikiri*, I can't but utter, "Wow, this is so good!"

*Every sushi restaurant has its own unique recipe for *nikiri shoyu* (*nikiri* for short), adding ingredients such as sake to pure soy sauce. It's known as the *Edomae*-style to serve nigiri after putting *nikiri* on the *tane* with a brush. Refer to page 204 for the Sukiyabashi Jiro *nikiri* recipe.

Back in the day in Tokyo, at sushi restaurants, chefs switched from using *kohada* to *koaji* (small horse mackerel) as it got warmer. It was still the same way when I started my apprenticeship at Yoshino at the late age of twenty-six, in 1951, after working at a small restaurant in Hamamatsu after World War II.

I wonder when sushi chefs started to use *kohada* in the middle of summer.

I think there is a desire on the customers' side to eat delicious *kohada* all year round. Moreover, there is an illusion that they can eat tasteful ones in summer; that's outside of its season. Supply has to follow demand. Therefore, we as sushi chefs have no choice but to search endlessly for ones that are delicious all year round.

In the days when I started my apprenticeship, in the season when *koaji* started to appear, *kohada* from the sea near Tokyo grew into the *konoshiro* size. So they used *koaji*. Back then, sushi chefs in Tokyo got their *kohada* from Chiba. The northern limit of the *kohada* they went for was Chiba; I'd never heard of the ones from Ibaraki.

For *shinko*, the furthest they were transported was from Atsumi Peninsula in Aichi Prefecture, and not only that, they appeared much later in the market than they do now.

Back then, it would have taken such a long time to ship from Kyushu, and it wouldn't have lasted even on ice. Even the *shinko* from Atsumi was transported after they grew bigger, so the beginning of August was the earliest we could make them into nigiri.

Lately, they appear in the middle of July. The first ones are from Maisaka (Shizuoka). Sometimes, there is nigiri with four very small *shinko*, but back in the day, people must have trashed them at the market since they didn't know what to do with such tiny ones. By the time these small fish got to the Tsukiji market, their stomach had melted, and they were useless.

But now, it's the motorization era. After 1970, styrofoam came into wide use, and it does a great job of keeping the contents cool. And if it's early *shinko*, then you can sell just one box for a surprisingly high price. That's why they transport it even if it's one kilogram. If it were *iwashi* (sardine), then no matter how much the market price rose, they'd have to sell many boxes to make the same amount of profit.

That's why *shinko*'s arrival is rapidly getting earlier.

By the way, first *shinko* at its most expensive cost 60,000 yen per kilogram, on July 12, 1996. One *shinko* at that cost-price is roughly 600 yen. And this was a two-slice-topping size, so for two pieces of nigiri, the cost was four times that. Of course, we don't add any fee for the hassle, which is ten times worse than for one-slice-topping *kohada*.

So when a guest who's a stickler about *shinko* comes to my restaurant, I'm tempted to joke about how much it cost.

"This is a real season-first, so when I calculate the cost, it comes out to 2,400 yen for a pair of nigiri. And that's just for the *neta*."

Of course, I don't actually say that.

"Oh, then I won't order."

That conversation would be a killjoy.

Well, it's not like we charge that much. This is a true statement. We charge 500 yen for one *kan* (piece) of *shinko* or *kohada* as always. We can't possibly charge more for a mere *kohada* nigiri.

"Why do you make them if you're losing money?" people often ask me, but it concerns my pride as a craftsman, and I ignore whether we're making or losing money in this case. Because the year's *kohada* starts with the *shinko* today.

"Goddamn it, here we go, this is this year's *shinko*!"

I make it with that kind of resolve.

In fact, regarding *shinko* prices, they were very expensive in 1995 as well. It was in the 60,000-yen range per kilo two years in a row. But the first *shinko* of the season in 1997 was 35,000 yen per kilo, so there must have been many restaurants that made *shinko* nigiri. It was still expensive, but I was relieved that I wasn't being as pigheaded as a result.

I just said that "*Kohada* is around all year," but as you know, its season is early autumn to winter. So why is it that delicious *kohada* comes to market all year around?

That's a true mystery. Japan is a narrow and long country; there's such a thing as "it's in season here," "not yet in season there," but the spawning season is very close everywhere. There is no way that *kohada* spawns in August in Hokkaido and March in Kyushu.

I would understand if the *kohada* from Mikawa (Aichi), which I consider to be the best in Japan, appears half a month later than the ones from Kyushu in the south. But when the ones from Mikawa come in, the ones from Kyushu haven't even materialized yet.

Lately, the first ones are from Maisaka, then the next are from Bentenjima, which neighbors to the west, but you can't continuously catch them. After they appear once or twice, somehow it's Mikawa or Atsumi. There is no way fish that tiny travel in a stream from somewhere around Lake Hamana to the ocean in Aichi. And a little while later, they appear farther offshore of Mikawa, and by then they've grown to their one-slice-topping sizes.

However, in Kyushu right around the same time, it's still *shinko*. From an amateur point of view, it should be the opposite. Because the seas around Kyushu are far warmer.

I pondered why it ends up being that way.

The conclusion after thinking it out very hard is as follows.

"*Kohada* is a semiannual-crop fish."

If *kohada* spawn twice a year following this theory, it makes sense. It does make sense, but then *shinko* should appear twice a year. If not, then the "double crop theory" doesn't hold up.

When it comes to the logic, to be honest I don't get it at all. Once the ones from Mikawa appear, the next ones are from Kyushu, but then it's strange that the ones from the interim don't come in so much.

On top of that, it's incomprehensible that there are *kohada* from Kyushu of a size I can make into one-slice-topping nigiri almost all year round.

"It's gotten colder, so why are we seeing such cute little ones around now?"

"Fish usually have a set spawning period, but to tell you the truth, this one must have been born late and out of wedlock."

I'm being silly saying stuff like that, but I don't see any rhyme or reason at all.

I still have a lot to learn, even now that I'm over seventy.

Silver-Skinned Fish: *Iwashi*
No other fish tastes so different in and out of season

I haven't heard of any sushi restaurant in Tokyo that features nigiri with phenomenal raw *iwashi* (sardine) as its selling point. The higher class the sushi restaurant, the more strongly they must feel that "We can't serve such a low-grade fish."

Another reason they wouldn't want to serve *iwashi* is because it's hard to keep it fresh. And you can't charge too much for mere *iwashi*, so the cost doesn't balance out with the hassle.

Iwashi goes bad really quickly in any case. If we just throw it into the *neta* case, the red muscle oxidizes and turns black, so first thing in the morning, we finish frantically taking care of the head and the innards, then painstakingly wash it with salt water and soak it in ice. If we don't work on it that much, we can't keep it fresh until nighttime.

Also, refrigerators dry the fish and make it lose its freshness. Therefore, we put it in a *hyozoko* (box with a large block of ice). You remember when Tokyo had the water shortage, and there was a commotion that "We can't get ahold of ice." That time, we bought a special fridge that prevents dryness. There is no other fish whose care is so troublesome.

There is yet another tough condition: I can't serve it to our guests unless it's the finest quality *iwashi,* matching that of our *kinkai hon maguro, anago, aka gai,* and such. The discrepancy would be an issue.

So I chose *maiwashi* caught by day-trip boats that leave the port in the morning and return in the evening. To sum up, they are medium and large ones landed on Choshi (Boso Peninsula) and Misaki (Miura Peninsula). Especially the large ones have to be fat like Konishiki (a popular sumo wrestler from overseas), otherwise we can't use it, so without exception our customers who see our *neta* box say, "This is the first time in my life I've seen it so fat."

However, the one in the *neta* box is for display. After we receive an order, we take out *iwashi* that's been soaked in ice cubes in the *hyozoko*. It's only then that we open the fish with our hands and make nigiri.

With plump in-season *iwashi,* the fatty layer in between the skin and the flesh is amazingly thick. Despite that, it neither smells fishy nor tastes greasy. The contrast between the pure white of the fatty layer and the bright red of the dark meat is remarkably beautiful when I slice the freshest ones. After I make the nigiri and brush *nikiri* on it, the colors are brought to life even more.

"What's going to happen to the display fish in the *tane* box?" our guests often ask us.

We cook it and eat it later.

When it's simmered, it's so delicious that I think this particular joy is the reason I continue to be a sushi chef. I can taste the fish especially well when it's simmered. If I cook one out of season, it tastes only salty, but for in-season *iwashi* that has put on fat, the deliciousness is brought out so much that I tilt my head and wonder, "Why in the world does it taste so good?" A different

49

flavor is brought out compared to when it's raw.

Every time I finish eating hot simmered *iwashi*, I feel from the bottom of my heart: "This is the privilege of a sushi restaurant owner."

By the way, no other fish's taste changes so drastically in and out of season. You can find it at the market throughout the year, but I only make nigiri when it is in season. In a typical year, medium-sized ones that taste better start to appear in Tokyo Bay around mid-April. They stay medium-sized for about two and a half months. The fatty layer is still thin around this time; they have a smooth and soft taste. They start to gain a lot of fat right before entering the rainy season and grow into their round and plump large size. They taste the best right after the rainy season.

Of course the large ones have a stronger taste, but if you ask me which one tastes better, I don't think there is much of a difference. Large as large, medium as medium, they both have plenty of their own flavors and umami.

Iwashi finishes decorating our *neta* box in November. We don't use it after the beginning of December. It becomes skinny when it's in the spawning phase, and only the head is big. If you eat fish like that, small bones keep sticking inside your mouth—not good at all.

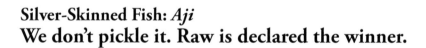

Silver-Skinned Fish: *Aji*
We don't pickle it. Raw is declared the winner.

While the currently popular *seki aji* ('seki horse mackerel from Saganoseki, Oita) has started to come into Tsukiji Market, what I really want to make nigiri with is *aji* (*maaji*), which is much smaller and tastes lighter.

Aji from Odawara (Sagami Bay) is the best that I can get ahold of in Tokyo. However, they barely come into Tsukiji lately. Even if they do, it's only a handful.

They do land. They land a little, but the local Japanese restaurants and dried food stores buy them out. They can sell them for a lot even as dried fish. One slice of a domestic wild one costs 400 yen. But the ones from Sagami Bay cost 800 yen. No wonder it's "the Phantom *Aji*."

The *aji* from Odawara are known for their slight sweetness, light aroma, and refined fat. Because the fat is spread equally, the flesh is whitish, so you know it's from Sagami Bay just from slicing it. It's superb fish.

And yet, it's not greasy. When you chew on it, the umami fully spreads in the mouth. One time, I made nigiri saying "so good, so good" and had thirteen pieces and still didn't tire of the taste.

However, sushi restaurant masters can't make nigiri with "the Phantom." What I use at the moment is mainly from Futtsu (Boso Peninsula)—the best quality if you don't count the ones from Odawara. Tokyo Bay and Sagami Bay are very close, so there is not much difference in taste.

Its season is from April to June, and it tastes the best in Tokyo over the summer. *Aji* starts to appear later in warmer Kyushu, just like *kohada*.

We don't pickle it. If you make nigiri with pickled *aji* and raw *aji* and ask me which one tastes better, there's no question I'll declare raw the winner. That's what I believe from comparing the tastes.

The reason sushi restaurants in the past pickled it is because it wouldn't be fresh. They salted it for half an hour with its skin on, pickled it in vinegar for half an hour, and when it came to making nigiri, they always paired it with the *oboro* (ground and cooked flesh) of whitefish or shrimp. *Aji* has a soft texture and soaks up vinegar quickly. Having pickled it for half an hour, the sourness stood out too much. That's why they sandwiched sweet *oboro*.

Raw *aji* is a very difficult *neta* to make nigiri with. Because of the grated ginger juice that accompanies it, the compatibility between *neta* and *shari* (vinegared rice) declines, and they start to fight, by slipping, when I try to make nigiri. It would be easy if I drained the excess liquid. Even a greenhorn could do it then. But the gritty fiber texture would remain on the tongue and the flavor would skip town. It's the nigiri pro who can make it right with juicy ginger in between.

Sukiyabashi Jiro master Jiro Ono never stops putting
in the effort to serve the best nigiri.
He works in silence, but he actually likes to talk.

Whitefish: *Mako Garei, Fukko*
Colored Fish: *Shima Aji, Inada*
Enjoy the light flavor and subtle taste difference

There is no better whitefish than *mako garei* (marbled sole) from Joban (Fukushima) in the warmer months. I believe in this. *Hoshi garei* (starry flounder), considered "the King of Whitefish," is in season too, but the drawback is that its flesh tightens quickly.

For instance, let's say, in the morning, there are *mako* and *hoshi garei* here, and we prep them the same. The *mako*'s meat is so resilient that in the evening, it's still live and fresh. However, the *hoshi* starts to turn white from its tail. The meat starts to die quickly. So I can't agree that *hoshi* is worthy of all the buzz.

Suppose we asked a hundred people who like whitefish, "Which one is *mako* and which one *hoshi*?" after letting them try both. I don't think there are many people who can discern the difference and say, "The *mako*'s flesh has a masculine texture and is on the plain side. In comparison, the *hoshi* tastes a bit over-rich and is slightly greasy, although of course it's whitefish, so it's not too strong."

There may not be any other sushi craftsman who values *mako garei* as much as I do. Because *hoshi garei* is a phantom fish that barely comes into Tsukiji, customers around Ginza probably know that it's very pricey and exclusive. However, if I, who've been running Sukiyabashi Jiro since 1966, am asked which I use in spring and summer, my answer is definitely "*Mako garei!*"

I valued *mako* even before anyone was using it. I've always thought, "This is good!" When I was entrusted to run Yoshino's Sukiyabashi branch in the late '50s, the whitefish in the warmer months were *fukko* (young sea bass), *suzuki* (Japanese sea bass), *kochi* (flathead), and *soge* (young flounder). Because I've been like this, I may be overrating it.

53

You know, it's not like I don't value *hoshi garei*. I think highly of it, but if it's a question of which one to use, then...

I guess that's what evaluating means.

Of course, the *mako*, whose meat is more than sufficiently robust, also has a weakness. Unlike *hirame* (flounder), the *mako's engawa* (little flesh on the fin) tastes bad. It has a grassy and fishy flavor. And it would be rude to serve that to our guests, so we don't. We store them in the freezer and only the restaurant staff eats it.

I try to finish using *mako* on the same day while its meat is still live and fresh. It's the responsibility of the sushi maker, but especially with whitefish we need to make nigiri while it's at its prime to eat. And we have to change the thickness of the slice between those that are too fresh and those that taste mature after a little while. With the ones that are too fresh, if you don't slice them thin, they get chewy, and on the other hand, the mature ones' umami is only brought out by being sliced slightly thicker. This slight thickness is a matter of one millimeter. But the subtle difference decides the taste of whitefish.

I do make nigiri with *fukko* (young sea bass) in early spring. If *mako* is a masculine fish, then *fukko,* with its soft tissue, is feminine. *Fukko* that time of year is not cheap at all. But you see, when I make nigiri with *fukko* and then with *mako*, everyone says, "The *mako* tastes better." Same thing with *suzuki* (Japanese sea bass), but in that case, they must be responding to the pushy flavor as soon as they put it in their mouth.

Fukko is somewhat pushy not only on the belly but also on the back, where it's supposed to taste plain. There are not many fish that can live in both seawater and freshwater that taste good. This, of course, applies to raw *suzuki* too. I completely understand why people of old invented *arai* (slicing whitefish very thin and soaking it in either cold water or ice). If you eat it with *sumiso* (miso with vinegar), the pushiness disappears, and you don't balk at the flavor.

On the contrary, *mako garei* doesn't have a shortcoming like that. It has a smooth and natural flavor.

There is a problem with *shima aji* (striped jack). Well, actually the problem is not with the *shima aji* but the guests who order it. What I mean to say is that back in the day, they only ate wild-caught fish so they knew its real flavor.

Meanwhile, what today's guests remember on their tongue is farm-raised fish, so even if I make nigiri with the most delicious wild *shima aji*, their reaction is: "Too plain, not satisfying."

The same is true of *inada* (young yellowtail), so young customers especially say, "It doesn't taste good. It doesn't have any flavor. It's just chewy." People nowadays are used to eating *ikezukuri* (raw fish prepared alive) of farmed *hamachi*. It's firm to the bite and yet very fatty. This is why when I make nigiri with wild *inada*, they react with, "What the heck is this?"

It's not fatty, but it's chewy, it's sinewy, and thus hard to eat for them. But that's not it, at all. The same goes for *shima aji* (striped jack), but we could almost call it *shiromi* (whitefish) for its plain and delicious taste though its flesh has color and is categorized as *iromono* (colored fish).

And so, once in a while, when I see *inada* I like, I make nigiri with it. It has a clean, plain, and light flavor; you can enjoy the taste in season twice a year, in spring and early winter.

Ika: Koika, Aori Ika
Aori ika is a sake side. *Sumi ika* is for nigiri.

The *koika* (small squid—offspring of *sumi ika*, "ink" squid) that start to appear in August remind sushi chefs that autumn is approaching.

That's because *sumi ika*'s growth rate is very fast. In the small squid period, its size is small enough for *maruzuke*, one squid for one nigiri, and later *warizuke*, one squid for two pieces of nigiri, but by the time summer is over and autumn deepens, it'll grow to be as big as the *sumi ika* you find in the fish section. So if you miss the chance, you won't be able to eat it until the following year. And this is why many people wait anxiously, saying, "Is it here yet? Is it here yet?"

When I make nigiri with *koika*'s translucent and thin flesh, you can see the green color of wasabi to whet your appetite. It certainly lacks the *sumi ika*'s characteristic firmness and rich flavor, but instead it has a fragile texture and sweetness, and it is also beautiful in its nigiri form when I use it as *maruzuke*.

To take advantage of these characteristics, it's important to keep it fresh. For that, prep it quickly in the morning and use it up on the same day. If you keep it until the next day, the nice translucent flesh turns pure white, and it becomes chewy.

Regardless, I don't like the price. It's not like *shinko* in 1996, which cost 60,000 yen per kilo for the first catch of the season, but it gets more expensive as the years pass by.

Sumi ika is the best as a sushi topping for its mouthfeel and balance with the vinegared rice. I think so.

Expensive *aori ika* (bigfin reef squid) is delicious as sashimi. Hence it's called "the King of Summertime *Ika*," but how about when we think of it as a nigiri topping?

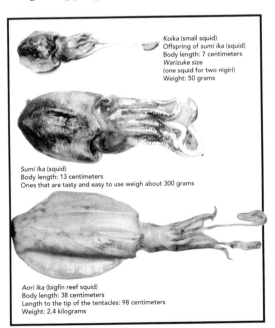

Koika (small squid)
Offspring of *sumi ika* (squid)
Body length: 7 centimeters
Warizuke size
(one squid for two nigiri)
Weight: 50 grams

Sumi Ika (squid)
Body length: 13 centimeters
Ones that are tasty and easy to use weigh about 300 grams

Aori Ika (bigfin reef squid)
Body length: 38 centimeters
Length to the tip of the tentacles: 98 centimeters
Weight: 2.4 kilograms

At our restaurant, we use live *aori* that's been swimming in the *ikesu* (a fish tank), so the flesh is extra firm. When I make nigiri, it doesn't curve softly along the *shari* (vinegared rice). That squid sweetness isn't brought out until you chew on it for a while in its sashimi form, cut in thin, string-like pieces. The umami finally comes out then. That's what I think, so unless it's a specific order, I use *sumi ika* for *shari*-hugging nigiri, and *aori ika* as a sake side.

For *geso* (tentacles), I only use *koika*. And in addition, I only make nigiri with very small ones. One piece of tentacle for one piece of nigiri. If it's bigger than that, it doesn't taste good when I make nigiri with it. It doesn't taste good even grilled. I'd decline serving it, saying, "Yes, we do have it, but I wouldn't recommend it."

We could make money if we obediently offered our guests what they want. However, I don't want to recommend something that I know doesn't taste good, telling them, "How about *sumi ika*'s *geso*? It's a bit firm, but the flavor will start to come out as you chew more."

This is the reason a lot of *geso* go into the stomachs of our young staff in autumn. Come to think of it, tons of it were served at lunch yesterday.

I don't make nigiri with *aori ika*'s *geso*. We broil it with soy sauce and serve it as a snack. It's better to broil it quickly than to make nigiri with it. I think so.

I don't refuse if a customer insists, "I still want you to make nigiri with it." But I can't make nigiri with it as is. It's too big to be a sushi *neta*, so I open it and then make nigiri with it. If it's too big, *geso*'s flavor is too strong and it overwhelms the *shari*.

Shellfish: *Tori Gai*
Edomae-style *tori gai*, I could never forget about it

The place that produced the best-tasting shellfish in Japan back in the day was Tokyo Bay. But the habitat of shellfish is now all reclaimed. The same thing with Kemigawa in Chiba, where since the Edo period we used to catch *aka gai* (surf clam). *Kemigawa* used to be synonymous with *aka gai*.

We used to be able to catch *miru gai* (geoduck clam), too, as well as *hamaguri* (hard clam) and *baka gai* (*aoyagi*/yellow tongue surf clam). They tasted far better than the ones from any other places. The *kobashira* (small scallops) were also the best.

Well, *Edomae*-style *kobashira* still taste good, even now. But the pieces have gotten smaller. I don't mind that they're smaller, but they also have sand, and we can't seem to get rid of it no matter what. We end up ruining half of it as we try to get rid of the sand, so we switched to using *ohoshi* (bigger *kobashira*) from Aomori or Hokkaido.

I can't seem to forget about the *Edomae*-style *tori gai* (cockles). The big ones were as thick as 1.5 centimeters, and they were fluffy like a carpet. *Tori gai* nowadays at its biggest comes at six pieces per box, but it used to be just three. That's how magnificent they were. I couldn't make nigiri with it unless I sliced it into three pieces, but it was so soft. When shellfish gets too big it's usually very firm, but these weren't tough at all. They also had plenty of sweetness and aroma.

We have only one guest left who's tasted it. When the *tori gai* season comes, this guest, who's more than a dozen years younger than me, always says, "*Tori gai* nowadays…" There are only two of us who remember that taste—just the gentleman and myself.

It's all in the past, but not ancient times. I'm talking from about 1970 to 1975.

What I mainly use now is from the Atsumi Peninsula. Although it's not as great as the *Edomae* catches from the old days, I can start to get big, good-quality ones in late April. I can't make nigiri with it as is, so I slice it into two pieces. It's that big.

In any case, the staff at shellfish stores are skilled professionals. They lightly boil the *tori gai* and finish them so they feel a bit raw, soft and sweet. Shellfish from other places are a bit firmer, so I always end up buying the ones from Atsumi.

When handling *tori gai*, you have to peel it without losing the unique coloring on the surface, and then bring out its inherent sweetness and texture by adjusting how much to boil it. This is how the flavor is set, and why the peeling and boiling method is a trade secret. When the fishmongers get to work, they lock the shack and don't allow in any strangers.

It must be a somewhat bizarre sight.

Simmered Item: *Awabi*
The *ohara* is a very mysterious *awabi*

The traditional work done by sushi chefs to *awabi* (abalone) is *nikkorogashi*. When you roll it around in the pot with boiled-down soy sauce and sake, it turns into shiny, red-and-black simmered shellfish. But if you make it that way, good *awabi* becomes too hard.

That's why I slice it thinly and make nigiri. But whether it's hard or soft, if you brush on the strongly flavored *nitsume** that's the standard accompaniment for simmered *neta*, two-thirds of the subtle and sensitive aroma will be gone. If you were to make nigiri with *nikkorogashi*, you wouldn't have to look desperately for scarce *awabi* from Boshu or Ohara like me.

**Nitsume* typically is a broth that comes from simmering *anago* (conger eel). Back in the day, they used a combined *nitsume* made from *hamaguri* (hard clam), *anago* (conger eel), *awabi* (abalone), etc., for the same gamut of *nimono-dane* (simmered toppings), but today, it's common to use *nitsume* made with *anago* for all of them. Find the Sukiyabashi Jiro recipe on page 204.

However, my steamed *awabi* couldn't possibly be made without using the soft female shellfish from Ohara, the so-called *biwakkai*. Why?

"I feel like I'm tasting a supremely blissful extract of the ocean. Its overwhelming deliciousness and sweet aroma wash away everything bad that I've ever tasted in the past."

A familiar face at my restaurant even put it in such a literary way, because the tender mouthfeel, the moistness when it goes down the throat, and the sweet aroma as if it's the milk of the sea are by far the best with *biwakkai* from Ohara.

As a sushi ingredient, *awabi* must be cooked and not used raw. That's what I think. Especially with the firm *aokkai* (male shellfish), it's nice to eat as *mizugai*, which is cut in cubes and then soaked in ginger vinegar, but it's too crunchy for nigiri. So if a customer orders a raw nigiri, then I use *biwakkai*, which has the soft flesh and the strong aroma of the sea.

If you have it raw, it doesn't make a big difference whether it's from Boshu or other places. It's when you cook it that you feel a huge difference. If you simmer *awabi* from other places, all of its inherent character and the rich flavor escape, and it becomes hollow. On the other hand, the *ohara* turns indescribably moist when cooked.

Whenever I slice the *ohara*, I wipe the knife every time. The blade becomes dull because the *ohara*'s amazingly rich gelatinous layer sticks to the knife. I think it's this gelatinous layer that creates the world of difference in taste.

My steamed *awabi* has a similar taste to the *mochi awabi* that they make in *kappo* (high-end traditional cuisine). But I don't actually steam it, I simmer it in a half-sake, half-water sauce for about three and a half hours, which brings out the flavor. So it's like *sakani* (simmering in sake), and what matters is how to bring out the natural flavors of the ingredient.

I want to prioritize preserving the aroma of the milk of the sea over everything else, so I brush not the thick and sweet *nitsume*, but the light *nikiri shoyu* on nigiri.

I'm not certain why or when I started to make it that way. I remember experimenting with it, trying to make it a bit fluffier or to bring out more of the aroma. But because I'm the master of a sushi restaurant, not a scientist, I don't have lab notes as in "when I did this, this happened."

There are many people who say:

"Your *awabi* nigiri is immensely mysterious."

"I've never seen a nigiri with a steamed *awabi* that hugs the rice so perfectly."

"Normally, they put *nori* around it so it doesn't fall apart."

But I do think it's the natural way. *Shari* and *neta* together become one as nigiri. Am I wrong?

How to cut a steamed *awabi*

To use it as nigiri-*dane*, carve a concave edge.

A few minutes after carving it, the surface starts to form a convex curve. You then have to slice according to the convex shape.

To reveal a trick, when I cut at the surface, I use the knife to carve a con-cave shape so that it'll curve along the *shari*. And this is the mysterious part, but the flesh of the steamed *awabi* with a dent in the center starts to bend powerfully back out, as if it's alive. The heat was applied to it for three and a half hours to four hours, so there is no way it's still alive. The *ohara* is a very mysterious *awabi*.

Unfortunately, they instituted a fishing ban on the *ohara* in 1995, effective for five years, until 1999.* It got too popular and became scarce.

I was thinking, "This is a problem," but then I found out that with *biwa-kkai* caught in Iwawada, which is very close to Ohara, I can make *sakamushi* (a dish cooked in sake) that compares favorably. Maybe because the *biwakkai* eat *kajime* (ecklonia cava) like the *ohara* does, even their shells look very sim-ilar. I just don't believe they aren't related.

However, only a little comes around to Tsukiji, so even the *iwawada* has become scarce.

The *awabi* used to make the *sakamushi* is best for its flavor and softness at around 800 grams, and up to a one-kilogram weight, we can make delicious ones. If it's smaller, then it won't absorb the aromatic flavor of the broth, and if it's bigger than one kilo, then even if it's from Ohara or Iwawada it becomes too hard after simmering.

At this point in 1997, a reasonably sized *awabi* costs around 18,000 to 20,000 yen per kilo. In terms of how many pieces we can get out of it, we can't quite manage twenty, but after getting rid of the adductor, we end up with enough for about seventeen.

It's expensive, but there isn't much we can do about it since the *ohara* can't be fished. If I cared too much about the price, then I couldn't get ahold of it. For now, my priority is to secure the goods.

"If you have the *iwawada*, please share."

"How many do you want?"

"All of it."

---

*They normally remove bans after confirming the restoration of natural resources, but the fishing ban was extended after an investigation in 1999.

To make the *sakamushi*, I have to simmer at least three or four pieces of *awabi* to get the flavor, but lately, one or two pieces is all I can get ahold of. Back in the day, if I said, "I want ten pieces," it was easy to obtain them, but now that's a bygone dream.

Simmered Item: *Anago*
No, we don't broil our *anago*

Throughout the year, we use live *anago* from Nojima (Tokyo Bay, Kanagawa). The *nojima* is in a league of its own among *Edomae*; it's our huge attraction. It doesn't change much in taste throughout the four seasons, but from June to July it gets extra fatty and delicious.

After boiling it, we lay it on a tray on the counter and make nigiri at room temperature, then use it up on the same day. If we stored it in the fridge, the soft *nojima* turns hard.

No, we never broil it. If we broiled it, then the grilled aroma overwhelms its inherent delicate flavor. Plus, we don't finish our *anago* as something to be broiled.

It's really soft, so if we skewer it, the flesh falls apart. And if we were to broil it, we'd have to put it on a grill. We might be able to grill one side, but then it'd stick. If we peeled it off, then it would crumble. So this kind of argument occurs more than once a year: "Can you please broil it?" "I'm sorry, but we can't broil it." "Oh, don't say that, please broil it." "We can't broil it." "Then I don't want it." "Agreed, you're better off not ordering it." However, very occasionally I might suggest, "Would you like me to broil it?" That's when *anago* from another location jumped into the fish tank for the *nojima* at the market.

In early autumn, in the wee hours of the morning,
he rides his bike from Ginza to Tsukiji. The first job of the day is to
purchase ingredients; inevitably, he grows focused and tense.

Let's say there's a fish tank for the *nojima*, and a fish tank for *anago* from another domestic location, and both *anago* are swimming. If an energetic domestic one jumped into the fish tank for the *nojima*, even a pro who has dedicated his life to *anago* won't be able to tell the difference. Because there won't be any writing on its body saying, "I'm not a *nojima*."

Stare at it at the broker's fish tank—I don't know yet.

Touch a round, fat, and lively one.

I still don't know.

Choose.

I still don't know.

Drain blood from it.

I still don't know.

Open it after returning to the restaurant.

I still don't know.

The moment I know clearly is right after I boil it. The flesh is hard. Because there isn't much fat on it, it gets hard after being boiled for the same amount of time as the *nojima*.

The *nojima* is really soft, so if you don't gently lift it up with both hands, it falls apart. If the *anago* isn't from Nojima, then you can dangle it holding its tail, and it'll be fine. They're that firm sometimes. On days when such *anago* come my way and I know it won't stick to the grill and I can broil it just fine, the conversation goes smoothly: "Please broil it." "Yes, yes."

However, even on days when we don't have *anago* we can broil, there is this particular longtime customer who shows up and adamantly insists, "I absolutely want you to broil it!" Not only has he been our patron since the opening of our restaurant, but he's older than me. Guests like him are like gods. And I can't disobey the oracle, so although it's extremely rare, it's not that I never broil the *nojima*.

But to be honest, I broil one from the day before that's been stored in our fridge for making side dishes. It's already tightened and firm, so even when I put it on strong flames, it doesn't fall apart.

I don't make nigiri with broiled *anago*. I slice it into thin strips, put it in a small bowl, and sprinkle a little bit of wasabi *shoyu* and toasted *nori* and serve it as a sake side.

"The grilled aroma goes very well with sake," the god, who imbibes a glass before having nigiri, squints his eyes with delight.

We have another older customer who is extremely fond of broiled *anago*, and he gets cranky if we don't broil it no matter what. If we don't have *anago* we can broil on the day of his reservation, then when we prep and boil *anago*, we take some out to broil before it's ready.

We normally boil our *anago* for about twenty-five minutes, but we take it out after fifteen minutes. That way, we can broil it without it sticking to the grill.

We already know that they're going to order it, and they're longtime regulars who're also older than me, so I give them special treatment. If I don't obey, I'll face divine punishment.

So the days I broil *anago* are the days I happen to grab *anago* that's not the *nojima* and those days when the scary gods visit. In short, it's an exception among exceptions.

Simmered Item (Marinated): *Shako*
I select only the ones with the roe and marinate them

Our *shako* (mantis shrimp) is extra large, plus it contains roe.

I select *shako* with roe because I like the soft and flaky texture myself. So I assume our guests aren't satisfied either if it isn't soft and flaky.

At the market, they sell male and female *shako* mixed in a small box. How, then, do we serve only female ones with roe?

The secret is I only pick the ones with roe. You can tell at a glance if they have roe or not, so I sort them: "the ones with roe in this box, and the ones without in that box." I've had a very long relationship with the *shako* fishmonger, so he lets me be.

It hasn't led him to say, "Jiro is overbearing." Because there must be more than a few sushi masters who think the opposite—"male *shako* that curves along *shari* is better for nigiri"—and also, whether it has roe or not, there are customers who just like *shako* as is. In fact, even at our restaurant, there are occasional guests who say, "It's nice as a sake side, but the roe's out of place on a nigiri."

So what I do when I take such an order is to touch the *shako* and pick one with little roe, or if it happens to be a day when I only have plump ones, I pretend that I didn't hear them. After many years as a sushi restaurant pops, you come by a certain level of guile.

Oh, by the way, a customer said something like this a while ago: "You specialize in making nigiri with *shako* with the roe, but there must be many male *shako* in the box too. Do you eat the leftover male *shako* for lunch?"

No, of course not.

One box contains seven to ten extra-large *shako*, and out of it, three at the most are female, and sometimes just one. So on average, two per box. If I bought ten boxes containing ten each for instance, only twenty would be with roe. We'd have to eat eighty males for lunch on a daily basis.

I wouldn't like that.

Shako should be marinated. There is *shako* that's more roe than meat, so it's more delicious to have it marinated than as is after the *shako* fishmonger boils it.

Umami first comes out of the crumbly roe after it's seasoned. So to bring out the *Edomae* soft and flaky texture, we marinate it in a subtly flavored combination of *shoyu* (soy sauce), *mirin* (sweet rice wine), and sugar. We call this process *tsukekomi*. But because the finished color is light, a lot of people think that it's just boiled.

Shako that's been marinated has to be drained. If it's too watery, then the foundation *shari* (vinegared rice) gets slippery and the *neta* won't align with it. The *shako* nigiri requires technical skill.

Koshiba (Tokyo Bay, Kanagawa) is the only place I get it from. Of course the ones from other places come to market, but they lack the umami the *Edomae shako* has. There is *shako* in this world that doesn't even taste good at all. The horrible ones neither feel crumbly in the mouth nor have the aroma of *shako*, which makes me want to complain, "Hey, you must be related to tofu!" There is sloppy *shako* that's like some king of snails. We have to select carefully based on where it's from and its quality.

Lean Meat: *Katsuo Modori* (returning) is greasy and lacks the refreshing quality

The only *katsuo* (bonito) nigiri I make is with *hatsu gatsuo* (the first bonito of the season) in spring, and I don't use *modori gatsuo* (returning bonito) in autumn, because *modori gatsuo* is too greasy. But when it starts to appear in the spring, the fatty layer is thin, and it has its characteristic light aroma that's very appealing.

Of course, without its fat, *katsuo* is rubbish. However, *katsuo* that doesn't have the delicate and refreshing aroma doesn't taste good, either. *Modori gatsuo* has a unique aroma to it, too, but it lacks the refreshing quality of the ones from early spring. That's the definitive difference, and it's like fresh greenery and autumn foliage, or cherry blossoms and chrysanthemums.

The *hatsu gatsuo* fished off the Boso Peninsula in mid-April has a slight, cherry-blossom-like "this is spring!" aroma. *Modori gatsuo* is too fragrant, like chrysanthemum.

Well, it's not that I'm saying, "*Modori* tastes bad." I think it does taste delicious with its fatty layer. I do think so, but *katsuo*'s charms aren't limited to its fat. Plus, there isn't any sense of novelty, just like *edamame* beans in September. There, it falls short of *katsuo* caught in early spring. And that's why I don't use *modori gatsuo*.

Also, when autumn arrives, the lean meat of choice is *maguro* (tuna).

Katsuo from early spring not only has a clean taste and the aroma of very brightly colored lean meat, but also a light fatty layer in between its skin and flesh as an asset. So I smoke the surface quickly, using brand-new straw, to soften its skin.

With a powerful gas stove, it gets cooked through, and the nice fat melts.

The flame from straw, on the other hand, has a gentle heat, so only the skin gets cooked. The smoke also gets rid of the slightly fishy smell. But we have to use brand-new straw, because with older straw, the mildew smell will transfer.

The challenge with *hatsu gatsuo* is that we can't tell the quality until it's opened. It's not like the *modori gatsuo* with consistent fat layers. Often, I get a good quality one today, and then tomorrow, I come across one where the fat is gone and it's just hard.

I decided only to buy one per day, so when I open it, and it's not up to par, we won't have any to make nigiri with that day. We eat it in the kitchen instead.

We buy one the next day and open it, and it's bad.

Nope. Have it in the kitchen.

We open one the day after that, and it's bad.

Nope. Have it in the kitchen.

We open one the day after again, and it's bad.

Nope. Have it in the kitchen.

However, we've been on a streak the past two years, and our batting average exceeded, hear this, .900. While the year before that it was .100 or .200 and we could only use three *katsuo* over the season, it decorated our *neta* box almost every day for the month and a half when *hatsu gatsuo* lands on Katsuura in Chiba or Choshi, from early April to mid-May.

The *shinko* (young gizzard shad) from Mikawa was good, the *mako* (marbled sole) from Joban was good, the *tori gai* (cockles) from Atsumi was good, the *iwashi* (sardine) from Choshi and Misaki was good—it was a really great spring for the master of a sushi restaurant.

Sukiyabashi Jiro
Nigiri-*dane* Calendar

	Month	JAN	FEB	MAR	APR	MAY	JUN	JUL	AUG	SEP	OCT	NOV	DEC	
LEAN MEAT	Hon Maguro (bluefin tuna)	←											→	Mainly the belly of *kinkai hon maguro*. It gets fattiest from late autumn to winter.
	Kuyu Maguro (air-transported tuna)		Feb →											In absence of *kinkai* (from Japanese seas), *kuro maguro* from Boston, LA, Mediterranean.
	Katsuo (bonito)				Early Apr ←→ Mid-May									If there is no satisfying *katsuo*, then a season without it.
WHITE-FISH	Hirame (flounder)				Apr ←							Nov →		When it gets frosty, *hirame* starts to gain fatty layers. At its best when amber.
	Soge (young flounder)									Mid-Sep ←→ Oct				Offspring weighing less than one kilo. Fills gap between *mako garei* and *hirame* weighing above two kilos.
	Mako Garei (marbled sole)				Mid-Apr ←					→ Mid-Sep				In contrast to *hirame*, a whitefish whose season is in summer. Nigiri not made with its *engawa*.
	Suzuki (Japanese sea bass), Fukko (young sea bass)				Apr / Fukko ←					→ Suzuki / Sep				Inner bay ones avoided as being too greasy. Nigiri with *fukko* or small *suzuki* beginning around June.

*The arrows in the chart show when the *tane* is acquired in season. The quality of nigiri-*dane* (topping) depends greatly on natural conditions each year. When a season arrives but the *neta* (ingredient) quality is bad, then no purchases are made, and there are times when a *neta's* season arrives earlier or later than usual. Please think of this chart as an approximate guide.

Month	JAN	FEB	MAR	APR	MAY	JUN	JUL	AUG	SEP	OCT	NOV	DEC	
COLORED FISH — *Shima Aji* (striped jack)					May			Aug					Only when wild ones are available. Unlike farmed ones, flesh is tighter and plainer.
Inada (young yellowtail)				Apr							Nov		Young *buri* before they start to wander around. Taxonomically considered lean, sushi restaurants categorize them as colored.
Shokko (young greater amberjack), *Kanpachi* (greater amberjack)			Mid-Mar	Shokko	Mid-May				Sep	Kanpachi / Oct			Young greater amberjack: tissue texture of the *buri* family, but tightens and fattens in the summer.
SILVER-SKINNED FISH — *Kohada* (gizzard shad)	←											→	Base size is *maruzuke* (one whole fish per nigiri). From June to July, sometimes *katamizuke* (one side of the fish per nigiri).
Shinko (young gizzard shad)							Mid-Jul	Aug					The size changes daily from four to three to two to one-and-a-half to one per nigiri.
Aji (horse mackerel)			Mar					Aug					The best come from Sagami Bay a few times during the year. Second best is Tokyo Bay.
Iwashi (sardine)				Mid-Apr / medium-sized			Mid-Jul / large-sized				Nov		Medium-sized's amount of fat best for nigiri. Fat ones recently scarce.
Saba (mackerel)		Feb									Nov		Only the plump ones. Good to eat after pickling and leaving overnight.
Sayori (halfbeak)	Jan									Oct			Bigger early in the year than in autumn and called *kannuki*.

Month	JAN	FEB	MAR	APR	MAY	JUN	JUL	AUG	SEP	OCT	NOV	DEC	Notes
SHELLFISH													
Aka Gai (surf clam)													Plump ones from Yuriage in Miyagi with the best aroma. While off-limits from Jul to Aug, the ones from Ise, Kyushu, and Kanonji.
Miru Gai (geoduck clam)													From Atsumi the best for aroma and sweetness. It and aka gai the champs among shellfish used for nigiri all year.
Tori Gai (cockles)				Apr	Mid-May								From Mikawa has black shiny surface, those with thick flesh selected.
Awabi (abalone)				Apr					Sep				For raw nigiri, easier-to-chew females better than males with tough flesh.
Kobashira (small scallops)													Large pale ones from Hokkaido, small orange ones from Futtsu or Ise.
SIMMERED ITEMS													
Anago (conger eel)													Only from Nojima. Ones that make three to four nigiri per fish have best amount of fat.
Mushi Awabi (steamed abalone)				Apr					Sep				Jiro's attraction, soft females from Ohara. While off-limits, comparable ones from Iwawada.
Shako (mantis shrimp)				Apr		Mid-Jun							Only from Koshiba, Yokohama, marinated. Only those with offspring, which makes it seasonal.
Hamaguri (hard clam)				4/10						Oct			Simmered and marinated, from autumn when they start to have offspring to early spring.
Tako (octopus)			Mar								Mid-Nov		Boiled on premise. From Sajima and between 1.5 to 1.8 kg for best aroma and firmness.

Month	JAN	FEB	MAR	APR	MAY	JUN	JUL	AUG	SEP	OCT	NOV	DEC	
IKA (squid), EBI (shrimp)													
Sumi Ika (squid)			←--------	Apr →					Sep ↓				Best when it makes four pieces. By March, big enough for eight pieces. Offspring of *sumi ika*. Mouthfeel
Koika (small squid)								Early Aug ←→	Early Sep				when big enough to make one or two nigiri is particular to the season.
Aori Ika (bigfin reef squid)					May ↕			Aug					Raw, it's particularly firm, best eaten as sashimi to enjoy the texture.
Geso (squid tentacles)								Early Aug ←→	Early Sep				Only of *koika* for nigiri. *Aori ika*'s recommended as hors d'oeuvre.
Kuruma Ebi (prawn)	↕												*Oguruma* from Tokyo Bay hard to acquire in consistent sizes.
MISCEL-LANEOUS													
Ikura (salmon roe)	↕												Marinated in soy sauce. Stocked up in bulk in fall when fished and rapidly frozen at -50° C.
Uni (sea urchin)	↕												*Shiro uni* from Hokkaido or Aomori with strong sweetness. Smooth creamier ones better.
Tamagoyaki (Japanese omelette)	↕												With ground *shiba ebi* and Japanese yam. Eggs from Okukuji. Each sheet cooked for forty minutes.

72

NIGIRI-*DANE* IN AUTUMN AND WINTER

Seafood in this chapter
Saba (mackerel), *Sayori* (halfbeak), *Sumi Ika* (squid), *Kuruma Ebi* (prawn), *Miru Gai* (geoduck clam), *Aka Gai* (surf clam), *Madako* (common octopus), *Hamaguri* (hard clam), *Hirame* (flounder), *Soge* (young flounder), *Aoyagi* (yellow tongue surf clam), *Hotate Gai* (scallop), *Taira Gai* (razor clam), *Buri* (yellowtail), *Tai* (sea bream)

"Since the old days, at sushi restaurants in Tokyo, whitefish in the colder months has meant flounder. I don't make nigiri with sea bream."

Kuruma ebi, tako, saba, hamaguri—the originality of a sushi restaurant is demonstrated first and foremost by its boiled and pickled *tane*, which are worked on with care. Excessive consumption of salt has gained attention as an issue lately, and sodium use has to be kept to a minimum. At the same time, the taste buds of regulars, who are mainly seniors with a discerning palate, need to be satisfied. A sushi restaurant master doesn't have it easy. Autumn, and then winter. The seasons are blissfully captured with a mouthful of seafood with plenty of fat on it.

Silver-Skinned Fish: *Saba*
Kan Saba (cold season mackerel) is really delicious. It's our main attraction.

Saba (mackerel) from Wakasa is a superior-quality item, on a different level from any other *saba*. However, it's considered to be a low-grade fish in Tokyo. Because everyone thinks this, only a few sushi restaurants pitch their *saba*. Even if they have it, it's like, "If you want, I'll make nigiri with it."

Fatty *shime saba* (pickled mackerel) is really delicious. I truly believe in this, so *kan saba* is one of our specialties. The *neta* is so popular that there's even a regular customer who finishes one side of the fish by himself like it's nothing.

At sushi restaurants in Tokyo, chefs normally leave the inside semi-raw, but I pickle it all the way through, much like *kizushi* (pickled sushi) from Kansai.

Of course, if I asked our guests how pickled they prefer it to be, I'm sure I'd get many different answers.

"I like it when the skin also feels raw."

"I prefer only the inside to be raw."

"I like it almost too pickled."

As a rule, I make nigiri with *saba* that I pickled the night before. With silver-skinned fish, if you don't let it rest for a certain amount of time after pickling, the inherent flavor won't come out. That's the cardinal rule for setting the flavor.

However, even though it's pickled, it's only good to eat for so long. The second day after it's pickled is good, and then it feels like it may be pickled a bit too much on the third day, and on the fourth day, it's not good anymore. The fat starts to oxidize, so we have it in our kitchen.

We actually had some for lunch yesterday. When we grill fish that's been pickled for too long and is sour, it has a different taste, and it's really delicious. I learned this *yaki shime saba* (grilled pickled mackerel) from someone from Tosa (Kochi Prefecture).

I only make nigiri with *saba* in the cold months, from November to February. In March, they start to have offspring, and their flavor declines. So they only decorate the *neta* box for at most four months. It's one of the *neta* that we have to stick to using in its season.

With *saba*, you don't need to bother where it's from all that much. In western Japan, you'd want it to be from Wakasa, but *saba* doesn't have much difference in quality in the first place. They swim in schools, and when you catch them in a net, if one is round and fat, then the whole batch is fat. You can catch good-quality *saba* in one swoop.

The best ones that come into Tsukiji are from off Choshi or the Miura Peninsula. In the past, good-quality *saba* came from the Sea of Japan, but we barely see them now. Their catches have dwindled, and supplying the Kansai region is probably the best they can do.

It's easy to evaluate its quality. Unlike *katsuo* that you have to open to assess, with *saba*, as long as it's stocky, round, and fat, it has a sufficient fatty layer. So we may eat the leftovers in our kitchen because we didn't sell them, but never because we chose wrong.

At a glance without opening it, I already know that a slim one's flesh is dry. If they only have *saba* like that, then we'd say, "We're not serving any today."

Although *saba* is one of our attractions, we only use one or two a day. I can't buy a whole box like fishmongers do, so I carefully choose the fattest fish out of the box. As long as I'm picking out just one, they won't say, "Jiro is a tyrant."

Say a whole box of premium-quality *saba* costs 20,000 yen for six to seven fish. If I paid 7,000 or 8,000 yen for two fish I like, then the cost of the box goes down.

The same thing can be said for *iwashi* (sardine) in the summertime. I only use up to ten *iwashi* per day, so I have to pick one by one. And even though it's only *iwashi*, a round fat one can cost 800 yen. Buying and serving loose fish is more expensive. If I buy ten *iwashi* for 8,000 yen, then the numbers end up uneven, but the price per box improves for them. That's why I'm not causing any troubles to fishmongers even when I pick the fish out one by one.

And that's why they say, "Jiro isn't being a tyrant."

I don't use *seki saba* (mackerel from Saganoseki, Oita), which isn't suited for pickling.

Silver-Skinned Fish: *Sayori*
I peel its skin right before making nigiri and use it raw

There are two seasons for *sayori* (halfbeak), spring and autumn. But there is a difference in fish size between the seasons, and the larger ones start to appear early in the year right before spawning. We call them *kannuki*, but there isn't much difference in taste.

Sayori is beautiful to look at. Some people may say its season is winter because, in some regions, it's indispensable as an item to bring good fortune for the New Year. That's the case for my hometown (Tenryu, Shizuoka Prefecture). We open the fish, debone it, roll it with ground flesh dyed red and blue, grill it in the shape of *noshi* (a traditional Japanese ceremonial decoration), and pack it in a *jubako* (a set of stacked boxes). For *suimono* (clear soup), we tie a thin strip of *sayori* and put it in.

Sayori has a blue back, so in the sushi restaurant categorization it's considered to be a silver-skinned fish, and in the past they prepared it with vinegar. However, the level of freshness now is different from the past. There is no need to kill its inherent plain yet rich flavor

Noshi Sayori
Layer the dyed ground flesh on the open *sayori* and roll it together. Skewer it and grill. When it's sliced after grilling, the cross-section resembles the letters *"no-shi"* (the word for a traditional Japanese ceremonial decoration).

with vinegar, so I sprinkle salt on it, rinse it with water, and then peel its skin right before making nigiri with it, raw. When it's raw, the tough skin stays in your mouth, so I peel it to make it easier to eat.

However, there are surely sushi masters who think that taking advantage of its beautiful silver skin is a must. On the day you buy the fish, you peel the skin and use it raw, and if there are leftovers, you put it through vinegar and make nigiri with the skin on. When *sayori* is rested overnight, the skin becomes softer, you see. That's one way. But I only use it raw, the day it's still live and fresh.

Sometimes a guest orders, "Sandwich some *oboro* (ground and cooked fish)." But our sweet *oboro*, made out of *shiba ebi* (shiba shrimp), needs to be paired with a well-vinegared silver-skinned fish, so it won't go well with raw *sayori*. What goes well with it, of course, is wasabi.

Ika: Sumi Ika
Texture, flavor, shape...the King of Squids

Koika (small squid) that's born in the height of summer grows bigger as it rains more. When it first appears, it's too frail to be used whole on nigiri, but as it grows to be the *neta* size for two to three pieces of nigiri, its sweetness and texture grow to match the typical characteristics of *sumi ika* (the "ink" squid).

As I mentioned, as a sushi *neta*, *sumi ika* surpasses summertime *aori ika* (bigfin reef squid). I do think so. It has a great texture because its fiber is so soft. If you chew on it a little, the *neta* and *shari* (vinegared rice) melt into each other for a refined flavor. When I place it onto our small black lacquered tray, the slightly blueish white nigiri glows. Wasabi showing through the translucent flesh is also appetite-stimulating. The *sumi ika* comes from Mikawa or Kyushu, and I choose ones that are as small as possible. A whole squid for six to eight pieces of nigiri would be the biggest. I don't use ones that are bigger than that.

I start using *koika* in mid-August, they grow to be *sumi ika,* and I stop using them after April. Until *koika* are born again, the *aori ika* (bigfin reef squid) takes center stage.

We don't use *yari ika* (spear squid), *aka ika* (neon flying squid), or *surume ika* (Japanese flying squid). Their flesh is too firm to make nigiri with them raw. We don't have *niika* (simmered squid) either. Nor do we do *inrozume,* which is stuffing rice mixed with *kanpyo* (dried gourd) and *gari* (pickled ginger) into a simmered *yari ika* (spear squid). It's probably because these items aren't traditionally *Edomae*-style. The master of Kyobashi did not teach me these things.

Ebi: Kuruma Ebi
Please have it at body temperature, not as *odori* (live)

A lot of great-quality sushi *neta* is caught in Tokyo Bay on the Kanagawa side: *shako* (mantis shrimp) from Koshiba, *anago* (conger eel) from Nojima, and the best *kuruma ebi* (prawn) from off Yokosuka. Futtsu on the opposite shore is not bad, but unfortunately their catches vary in quality and fall short in quantity.

The reason *Edomae*-style *ebi* (shrimp) is by far the best is that it's superior in criteria such as sweetness, aroma, and the color after boiling.

This is probably because there's plenty of food for them.

The seawater needs to be somewhat dirty for the *kuruma ebi*'s food to grow. "If the water is clean, *ebi* won't live there," so Tokyo Bay became its perfect habitat.

Although the seafood is back, it's true that Tokyo Bay still smells like oil. We can't use *fukko* (young sea bass) or *suzuki* (Japanese sea bass) that swim at the surface. As for *bora* (striped mullet), there is no way we could use it at all. However, *kuruma ebi,* which lives on the bottom of the ocean, doesn't smell like oil.

They are in season twice a year: in spring, when they become active after the seawater gets warmer, and from autumn to winter, when they start to absorb a lot of food to hibernate. I think the ones from spring are especially delicious.

When I peel the shell, if the fat from its *miso* (tomalley) gets on the cutting board, it's extremely difficult to wash off. The fat becomes that rich.

Some sushi chefs say, "Its season is summer." When the weather gets colder, *ebi* bury themselves in the sandy mud and hibernate, so these chefs say the season is summer based on the greater yield. For some reason, the *Edomae ebi* stopped hibernating, so they appear even in winter—I can make *Edomae*-style all year round.

The fishing method has also improved. In the past the fishermen used a tool that resembled a rake and caught *ebi* as if they were shoveling snow off a street. Sometimes we chefs couldn't use the *ebi* because their backs were scratched all over. But more recently, the fishermen stun the *ebi*, using electrodes to deliver a current in their habitat. They catch them in one swoop when *ebi* that were buried in the sand are startled and jump up.

So maybe it's not that the *Edomae kuruma ebi* doesn't hibernate, but instead it's forced out of its relaxing slumber by the electric shock.

After all, we're talking about a natural resource. We can't avoid days when we can't catch any, and then my go-to is from Lake Hamana. Until *kuruma ebi* returned to Tokyo Bay around 1985, I used the ones from Lake Hamana, which I believed to be the best in Japan. Compared to others, the wild *ebi* from Lake Hamana is still far better.

On a stormy day when there isn't even any catch from Lake Hamana, I use ones from Kyushu, for instance Shibushi Bay. But they just don't have as vivid a color as the ones from Tokyo Bay after boiling. When farmed *ebi* is boiled, the color comes out closer to yellow than red, and the wild *ebi* from Kyushu look similar to the farmed ones. And naturally, their sweetness and aroma are also faint.

Typically, at sushi restaurants in Tokyo, they make nigiri with *maki ebi* (small *kuruma ebi*) and use it whole, one per nigiri. But if I could say something, you can't taste the real deliciousness with *maki*, so I make nigiri with *oguruma* (large *kuruma ebi*). Or else, you can't enjoy the unique aroma and succulent sweetness and richness. It's so big that even a man can't put the whole piece in his mouth at once, so I slice one nigiri into two pieces before serving.

First and foremost, there is a difference in impact between serving *maki* and *kuruma*. I want to emphasize that it is the "bona fide authentic item." That is my thinking.

Kuruma ebi has become our big main attraction, but the reason I insist on using the wild variety, especially *Edomae* catches, is that I wanted to overturn the theory that *"Ebi* served in sushi restaurants don't taste good."

We can't do without *ebi* for *saramori* (plate of sushi) or *demae-zushi* (delivery sushi). However, everyone believes, "The taste doesn't matter as long as it's red, since they just need the red and white pattern of *ebi* to make *moriawase* (a plate of assorted sushi) look colorful." I didn't like this.

Of course, it has to do with the budget, too, but for some chefs, as long as it looks like *ebi*, it doesn't matter even if it's frozen. It doesn't matter even if it's finished (dead). It doesn't matter even if the tail is pitch black. Even if they use fresh *maki* from a tank, it doesn't matter if it's cold from being boiled once in the morning and nigiri is made with it late at night. Because of these practices, *ebi* became synonymous with dreck.

In truth, *ebi* is a supreme nigiri *neta* that deserves the best spot in *saramori*, because it's something that's naturally delicious. It's a great feast when you fry

Saru Ebi (hardback shrimp)
It was used for *oboro* until 1955. Not caught at all these days. The flesh was tougher than *shiba ebi*, but the coloring was vivid.

Shiba Ebi (shiba shrimp)
Used for *oboro* and *tamagoyaki* (Japanese omelette). Its distinctive feature is that the flesh doesn't get too hard after cooking.

Maki Ebi (prawn)
A type of *kuruma ebi* (prawn) that's typically said to be the best suited as nigiri-*dane*. Around 14 cm long.

Kuruma Ebi (prawn)
Used for *chirashi* (variety of toppings, mainly seafood, on a bed of rice) at *Jiro*. Around 17 cm long.

Oguruma Ebi (prawn)
Around 22 cm long. Weighs 50 grams. Used for nigiri at *Jiro*. The biggest *ebi* to be eaten as boiled shrimp.

fresh *saimaki* (young *kuruma ebi*) into tempura.

This is why I thought long and hard about how I could bring out its inherent flavor to the maximum as a nigiri *neta*.

"*Kuruma ebi* becomes a delicious *neta* after being cooked."

This is what was taught to me during my apprenticeship. But we also feast with our eyes with *Edomae*-style nigiri. So I wanted to perfect this beautiful *neta* with an even more vivid contrast of its red and white pattern.

I've tried many things, including different sources and altering the amount of time I boil it, and decided that *Edomae* is the best for boiling. Of course, even if it's *Edomae*, dead won't do. If it's not fresh and full of life, the natural *ebi* colorings won't come out.

The challenge is how to bring out its inherent flavor. I used to make nigiri twice a day with the ones that I boiled: at noon and at night. I thought that was the most delicious.

But five or six years ago, I was shocked when I happened to eat body-temperature *ebi*. It had a pronounced aroma and the rich sweetness. I couldn't believe that it was the same old *ebi*.

After that, I started to boil it after taking an order. It's done after five or so minutes of boiling, so all the guest has to do is to wait a little. This way, they can eat an extraordinarily delicious *kuruma ebi* nigiri.

When boiling, cook it through to its core and bring out all of the umami. And after boiling, blanch it to keep the coloring. But you mustn't chill it to its core. By the time the surface chills, the core is at body temperature.

This is the trick to bringing out the inherent flavor of *Edomae kuruma ebi* to the fullest.

After prepping it in the back, I bring it to the counter. It's boiled to a magnificently beautiful *ebi* coloring. These are the authentic natural colors created by nature. After peeling the shell and opening it, I make nigiri with it, and its flavor at body temperature, neither warm nor cool to the touch, is unparalleled. Its tomalley is especially delicious.

The boiled *ebi* in our *neta* box is for display. I don't make nigiri with it. We don't even eat it in our kitchen. We freeze it and mix it into our *shiba ebi* (shiba shrimp) *oboro*. With the natural coloring of *Edomae* catches, *oboro*'s color palette becomes even more vivid.

I don't make nigiri with *odori* (raw). Not even when one of our regulars orders it. Of course, if someone says, "I really want it no matter what," then we won't refuse to make nigiri with it. We keep all of our *kuruma ebi* alive and fresh. But for *Edomae*, it's more delicious to eat it boiled than raw. Naturally, food preferences are diverse. And since my business is about serving customers, I should make nigiri without giving lip. I do think so, but I also know that boiled *ebi* tastes far better, so I can't help but talk back and say, "Please have it boiled, not raw."

Shellfish: *Miru Gai*
It's one of these nigiri *neta* that you either love or hate

If it's *awabi* (abalone) that's exceptional in the summertime, then for the current season the *Ryo Yokozuna* (the two top sumo wrestling champions) of nigiri *neta* are *miru gai* and *aka gai*. They split the popularity at the counter as well. When you broil them quickly and make *tsukeyaki* (a marinating and grilling technique), they're peerless sake sides.

But if I may say so, *miru gai* looks faded in color, so when I make nigiri with it, it doesn't look good. The fresher it is, the more the meat bends backwards and the worse the nigiri shape.

There is also an issue with its unique aroma, and some guests avoid it saying, "The smell of the sea and the twang are too strong and don't go well with *shari*." But on the other hand, there are guests who like it so much that they order many pieces. It's a nigiri *neta* that you either love or hate.

And also, there is no other shellfish that produces so much waste. First of all, its *himo* (string) doesn't taste good. If I made *tsukeyaki* with *shoyu* (soy sauce), then it's somewhat edible, but at our restaurant, we trash it along with the *hashira* ("pillar" or adductor muscle) and don't use it. We don't even have it in our kitchen. I have never seen our young guys eat it either.

Plus, it's gotten surprisingly expensive. I use ones from either the Atsumi

Peninsula, Okayama, or Kyushu, but eight nigiri-worthy *miru gai* weighing 800 grams cost over 10,000 yen at times. Since an incident when a diver was attacked by a shark, they've had low stock, but that can't be the only reason it's priced that high. I believe someone is manipulating the price.

If stormy days continue for three to four days and no *aka gai* come into Tsukiji, even the *miru gai* that they keep in fish tanks somewhere disappear completely. As soon as it starts to come in intermittently, the price hikes up to 10,000 yen.

It's expensive enough on a regular day. Even when I think, "It's reasonable today," it costs about 7,000 to 8,000 yen and doesn't get cheaper than that. In any case, it's turned into a nigiri *neta* that's expensive and rare. But it's a popular *neta*. I can't not have it at our restaurant.

Shellfish: *Aka Gai*
I can tell that it's from Yuriage just by looking at its shell

My overall evaluation is that *aka gai* is superior to *miru gai* as a nigiri *neta* by a whole notch or two. Its nigiri shape is better. Its shiny coloring is better. Its texture is better. The aroma, better. The flavor, better. Above all, its *himo* (string) surpasses its parent. It's delicious as nigiri. Wrapped in *nori*, delicious once again. Sandwich it with cucumber, even more delicious.

Out of the *aka gai* that we can get ahold of at Tsukiji, the ones from Yuriage (Miyagi) are the best, and I can distinguish them just by looking at their shells. Also, no others have such plump flesh.

It's extremely thick, yet it's mysteriously soft. Its coloring is natural and elegant. Its texture and its aroma when you chew on it are wonderful. As soon as I slice into it, the aroma of the ocean fills up the air in the kitchen. At any rate, all the criteria are filled three and fourfold. And it's an appropriate size to make one piece of nigiri.

Its season is winter. However, we serve it all year round since there are a lot of requests. This didn't just start; ever since I began working at Kyobashi, sushi restaurants in Tokyo have used it in the summertime as well. There are seas where their fishing doesn't get prohibited.

In July and August, when fishing them is banned in Yuriage, the ones from Kyushu come into Tsukiji. The *aka gai* from Kyushu can't compete quality-wise or fetch high prices, so they only send it in the summertime when Yuriage is off-limits.

So in the summer, I use the ones from Ise or Kyushu, but the ones in 1997 were especially, unexpectedly good. The coloring of the flesh was beautiful, and with those hues, most people wouldn't have caught on if I said, "This is from Yuriage." But of course, the flesh is a bit thin. Even right after they've laid their eggs and the ban is lifted, the *yuriage* never comes in that thin. They simply don't taste the same.

I don't put it through vinegar. As soon as the order comes in, I peel its shell, then use it raw to make nigiri to keep the flavor. If it's pickled in vinegar, then the nice aroma of the sea will disappear. Before the war, to avoid food poisoning, they put all the nigiri *neta* through vinegar. They made nigiri with *maguro* (tuna) after marinating it in *zuke* (soy sauce marinade), and even whitefish was pickled in vinegar or with *kobu* (kelp). But by the time I started working at Kyobashi, we no longer put it through vinegar and made raw nigiri.

At any rate, it was *aka gai* from Tokyo Bay, which was right in front of us. It was at the best freshness. Around 1955, plenty of *aka gai* that was fluffy and soft landed. It was easy to chew on and was moist with no firmness and highly aromatic; the *aka gai* from *Edomae* had a wonderfully dreamy flavor.

Even against the Tokyo Bay catches back then, the *yuriage* compared favorably in terms of its coloring and the flesh's firmness, and it got increasingly popular. Just like the Berkshire pork from Satsuma that's lined up in supermarkets, now every store claims, "Our *aka gai* is from Yuriage."

This is why I worry about the future. Yuriage is said to be a fishing port with very strict fishing regulations, but I really hope they keep following those rules. If not, like *awabi* from Ohara, they'll have to prohibit fishing for a long time. It's gotten so popular that I worry needlessly about the future.

Simmered Item: *Madako*
The way I massage and boil it is a winner, I praise myself

The season of *madako* (common octopus) is winter. However, there are unexpectedly many people who believe it's perennial. When I get an order in the middle of summer and respond, "We don't have it, it's out of season," the customer makes a strange face. In fact, the skinny summer octopus tastes bad. It's less objectionable to buy *yudedako* (boiled octopus) at a fishmonger than to boil octopus in the summertime. Theirs is a frozen octopus that was boiled while it was still in season.

However, if sushi chefs want to make really good *tako* (octopus) nigiri, then they have to boil it themselves. At least, that's what I was taught by Kyobashi's master chef. I only boil octopus in its season, which is from mid-November to late March at the latest, with its fatter tentacles and heightened aroma and richness.

I use Miura Peninsula *tako* that weigh between 1.5 to 1.8 kilograms, not more than two, from Kurihara, Misaki, and such, but it has a great reputation and some guests even ask, "Is this from Akashi?" because the massaging and boiling method that I came up with is a real winner. Yes, I'm praising myself.

With *tako*, the timing for massaging it is important. If you massage it while it's still very fresh, then when it's done boiling, for some reason, a hollow space is created in the tentacles. So it's actually very difficult to assess when to kill it and when to boil it.

From around 1954 to 1960, after being ordered to become the master-for-hire in Osaka by Kyobashi's master chef, I was forced to realize how wonderful *tako* from Akashi is. Without having done anything special to it, if I massaged it in a normal way and boiled it in a normal way, the deliciousness and the richness came out whole. The pleasant resilience when I chewed on it was naturally inherent too. The Akashi *tako* back then was actually that amazing.

After boiling, an aroma that resembled refreshing chestnuts started to rise in the air. Some say, "Good *yudedako* smells like milk," but I used to think of the sweet smell of chestnuts.

However, with the local *tako* from Kanto, if I just massaged and boiled it in a normal way, it didn't taste good at all. It doesn't have the pleasant bite to it. Or the refreshing aroma. Or the sweetness.

I figured that I needed to work out a special plan if I were to boil *tako* from Kanto. What I finally understood after much trial and error is that the temperature affects the flavor of *tako*.

With *yudedako*, you should only eat it at body temperature when it's aromatic. At body temperature, *tako* from Kanto is not inferior to the *akashi*. But it can't be hotter. Or colder. If you ever put it in the fridge, then the aroma and the texture decline by half immediately, and it becomes the run-of-the-mill and trite *yudedako* again.

This is why I start to boil it after timing the arrival of regulars whom I want to serve it to. Once it's done, I hang it until it reaches body temperature and try to maintain the temperature. As it cools down, the curled tentacles start to straighten, and it becomes easier to turn into nigiri.

I pull a *kakushi-bouchou* (making hidden slices in an ingredient) for nigiri and place a little bit of sea salt and serve it. The sea salt brings out the sweetness and aroma of *yudedako*. I don't brush *nitsume* (reduction sauce), which is typically used with boiled items, since it will kill the nice chestnut aroma.

For my guests who like to drink sake before eating nigiri, if I have *tako* at body temperature, then I recommend *tako-butsu* (diced octopus pieces), which I serve along with sea salt. It's the best way to enjoy the flavor and texture of *yudedako*.

Young people these days may not know this, but there's a piece of wisdom that's been handed down: the tentacle tips of *tako* are toxic.

"There is only one poisonous *tako* out of tens of thousands, but when you do get that one, your body gets pins and needles like with *fugu* (blow fish) poisoning."

I used to hear this from fishermen in Akashi back in the day.

Fugu originally did not contain poison. However, their food contained poison, and as a result of it accumulating in the body, it turned lethal. The fact that wild *fugu* is more poisonous than farmed *fugu* is due to their diet.

I don't know the validity of it, but I understand it depends on the food they eat in the case of *tako* as well. But even if it contains poison, it's said to be limited to their tentacle tips. So I always cut away the tip of the curled tentacle and throw it away, though when I display the tentacle in our *neta* box it's not cut away.

I hear there are restaurants that serve it as a sake side saying, "The tentacle tip is a delicacy," and I wonder about them.

Simmered Item (Marinated): *Hamaguri*
You're doomed if you use Korean-import *hamaguri* as is

Hamaguri (hard clam) is a traditional *neta*. The reason people used it as a nigiri *neta* is that plenty of them were caught in Tokyo Bay.

However, there were many sushi restaurants that didn't. The cooking technique for *hamaguri* didn't spread because there were sushi masters who didn't know how themselves, and the apprentices who came to be trained didn't get to learn and couldn't make nigiri with it even when they returned home. So it never spread.

But lately, I hear that sushi restaurants are starting to serve it. This may be the effect of a gourmet book that claimed, "You can tell the level of the sushi restaurant by whether or not they serve *hamaguri*."

Shellfish tends to harden after simmering. I cook *hamaguri* quickly, and then soak it in a marinade called *hamazume*—a mixture of its own broth, sugar, *shoyu* (soy sauce) and *mirin* (sweet rice wine)—and then let it absorb the flavor. This practice of sushi chefs is called *tsukekomi*, and it's the same for *shako* (mantis shrimp).

Hamaguri comes from Shima and Kuwana. However, purely domestic ones are extremely scarce. Most of them are originally from Korea and were let loose for about half a year in the seas of Shima or Kuwana. Once they get accustomed to Japanese seas, their very firm flesh becomes soft, and the aroma and the favor start to be balanced. Still, it doesn't compare to the *Edomae* yield of the past.

But you're doomed if you use *hamaguri* imported from Korea as is. It's tasteless as if you're chewing rubber. But that's the thing's nature. Even if you're an expert at *tsukekomi*, you can't possibly soften such hard flesh. It's a shellfish that we can't really do much to, and I wonder why umami starts to come out of them as soon as you domesticate them in Japanese seas.

Whitefish: *Hirame, Soge*
When the flesh turns an amber color, their season arrives

No matter how good the weather is, the season for *mako garei* (marbled sole) is finished in early October. When that time comes we use *soge,* or young *hirame* (flounder), for a while, and then we wait for the *hirame* to fatten up. Up until April, when they start to hold eggs, is my favorite time to use the *hirame* from Aomori that I like.

Lately, however, as soon as the *mako garei* is done, it's the season for *hirame*, and there is no time for *soge*. Maybe it's because of global warming that the *mako* continues to taste great. I try buying *soge* as well, but when I eat them both and compare, the *mako* is far better, so I go back to using it. Those days continue.

The whitefish I use is *mako* from Joban and *hirame* from Aomori, but recently in the seas around Aomori, the temperature doesn't go down even when autumn arrives. Especially in 1996, it was four degrees (centigrade) warmer than usual. It must have been a little warmer yet in Joban; I got to use *mako* up until the end of October probably because of the water temperature.

When it gets frosty, *hirame* starts to gain a fatty layer and its flesh grows plump. And the white flesh turns an amber color. This coloring becomes the deciding factor for the flavor of *hirame*. When you dip amber-colored *hirame* into *shoyu* (soy sauce), a surprising amount of fat starts to spread in the small bowl. Its resilient texture, aroma, and flavor are a blessing of the season beyond words.

So although I truly believe that "the king of whitefish is not *hoshi garei* (starry flounder) but *mako garei*," hypothetically speaking, if *mako* from Joban and *hirame* from Aomori appeared at the same time in the same season, then I'd pick *hirame* from Aomori without hesitation. They have different seasons, summer and winter, so this would never happen, but *hirame* is far better.

Until 1975, there was no way to deliver live *hirame* from Aomori to Tsukiji. This is why we considered the ones from Sagami Bay to be the best, but compared to the *aomori*, they're inferior. And by the time the ones from Sagami Bay turn white, the *aomori* is still amber. In other words, the season is so long that there's no comparison.

We select *hirame* that weigh about two kilos and are rotund with ample flesh. It's not sinewy and has plenty of umami. If I killed it in the morning at the riverside, then by the evening it's good to use. Even at its biggest, we don't go over 2.2 to 2.3 kilograms, because beyond that, it's still too live to use for nigiri even by the evening after killing it in the morning. It just feels crunchy, and its inherent flavor can't be brought out. It becomes good to make nigiri with it at noon the next day. By the next evening, there is plenty of umami, but the flesh loses its firmness.

So what gives me a headache is the market's off days every other Wednesday. Shellfish is alive the next day so this is not a problem, but good whitefish should be slaughtered fresh—and also whitefish is one of our main attractions. I don't dare utter the words, "We don't have it today."

This is why I ask two managers at the broker to take turns and come in on their days off to unlock the shop, and I go to slaughter a *mako* or *hirame* that's swimming in their fish tank. I only buy one, but I've bought whitefish only from them, so I can ask for unreasonable favors.

I also buy *anago* (conger eel) on their days off. If it's not alive, then I can't cook it to be nice and fluffy, and *anago* is also our big attraction. I can't use a hard one from the previous day.

Of course, I don't advertise by bragging about how much trouble I go to behind the scenes, saying, "This *hirame* is so fresh because I went to the market this morning even though it was closed. See, I put in so much effort."

But if a guest asks me, "Tsukiji must be closed today, so how come this is so fresh?" then I don't think it's an issue to explain, "Well, actually…"

Depending on the day, there are times when we can't finish using the whitefish. But if the timing isn't right, I don't make nigiri with it.

"I have half of a fish left. What a waste. Heck, I'll use it tomorrow!" If I did anything like that, then I wouldn't be able to make delicious nigiri anymore.

So what I do with the leftover *hirame* is to bring it home and grill it with butter. My wife gets so happy, saying, "Oh! You're making *bataayaki* again!" Our grandchild loves *engawa* (little flesh on the fin) grilled with butter. Our grandchild also loves the lean meat of *maguro* (tuna) from Oma in Aomori Prefecture (see pictures on pp. 100–106) that we can't use at our restaurant because the color turned a little bit.

"Our grandchild has no appetite!" Even on days when my family is making a big fuss, the kid finishes the *oma* that's gaining popularity lately like it's nothing.

My family is quite happy that the economic bubble burst.

The reason I don't make nigiri with them.
Shellfish: *Aoyagi* (*Baka Gai*), *Hotate Gai*, *Taira Gai*
We end up eating them in our kitchen

I wouldn't mind serving *baka gai* (yellow tongue surf clam), but only if there is a good one. I used it once a few years ago, and I haven't made nigiri with it since. Maybe because it has too singular a taste. There are close to no guests who like *baka gai* at our restaurant, so even when we have any, we end up eating it ourselves.

There is one particular regular who can't eat shellfish with a singular taste; he's never ordered *miru gai* (geoduck clam), not even once. He also hates *baka gai*, which has a strong ocean aroma, so when he comes to our restaurant, he badmouths it endlessly.

"*Baka gai* is the most inferior shellfish. The only ones below it are *shijimi* (freshwater clams) and *asari* (short-neck clams), so *baka gai* is at the lowest rank as a nigiri *neta*. You really can't serve that sweet and gross-tasting shellfish. If you keep serving lots of *baka gai*, then this restaurant will make a profit. But you can't serve it. It'll lower the quality of this establishment."

Of course, this is irrational. But I can see what he's saying. Maybe I actually also feel the same way, so I don't want to use it.

I also have more shellfish that I don't make nigiri with.

First of all, *hotate gai* (scallop)—most of them are farmed, so it's not worth making nigiri with them.

I have a regular who says, "Make nigiri with *taira gai* (razor clam)."

I don't mind serving this shellfish. But it's not a *neta* with a strong flavor, so it's never going to be popular. We either fry it or grill it with butter and have it for lunch.

So what we eat in our kitchen is roughly as follows: *Taira gai*. *Katsuo* (bonito) that's not good after opening it. *Soge* (young flounder) that tastes worse than *mako garei* (marbled sole) and that we can't use. *Engawa* (little flesh on the fin) of *mako*. *Fukko* (young sea bass) after one day. *Geso* (tentacles) of *sumi ika* (squid) that's too big. Cold *tako* (octopus). Lean meat with a faded color. Leftover dead *anago* (conger eel). *Saba* (mackerel) that's pickled too much. *Aji* (horse mackerel) and *iwashi* (sardine) that went on display in our *neta* box. And *nakaochi* (leftover flesh on the spine of a fish).

To finish eating all of them is not easy. Even our young guys, with huge appetites, can't finish them. This is part of the reason we don't carry *neta* that we only serve occasionally.

The reason I don't make nigiri with it. Colored fish: *Buri*
The singular flavor and character of its flesh don't work well for nigiri

Kan buri (cold season yellowtail) from the Sea of Japan comes in sometimes. But at a small restaurant like ours that fits ten people at the counter, we can't finish using a ten-kilo *buri* (yellowtail). It's not whitefish, but a colored fish that has a slight tone to its flesh, so it darkens very quickly. So even if we slice it and see a nice color, by the time we display it in our *neta* box, the dark meat turns pitch black.

In the past, around when I became a sushi craftsman, Kyobashi's master chef made nigiri with *kan buri* in the winter. He bought the whole fish, but used only the belly part with lots of fat on it and didn't use the back part at all, and ate it in the kitchen. But he made a profit because unlike how it is now, it used to be a very cheap fish. Back then, it was far cheaper than *kinkai hon maguro* (bluefin tuna from the seas around Japan), which was also cheap at the time.

But the reason I don't serve *buri* is not because I'm concerned about making a profit. It has far too singular a flavor to be a nigiri *neta*. When I pair it with *shari* (vinegared rice), *buri* overwhelms it no matter what. But if I tried to slice it thin like *otoro* (fatty tuna), it throws off the balance between the top and the bottom. No matter how I approach it, it just doesn't become nigiri with a deeply impressive flavor.

I don't think of *buri* as a bad-tasting fish. When I visit Kanazawa in the winter, I actually have *kan buri*. I do have it, but it's best to eat the belly part as sashimi dipped in *shoga joyu* (ginger soy sauce), and I'd probably order it as teriyaki or *shioyaki* (salt-grilled). That's how it tastes good, and it's not for nigiri.

Of course, there are restaurants that sell *buri* nigiri as their attraction in the winter, and I know that there are customers who smack their lips over them. There are people in the world who swear, "The flesh from the tail of a shark as nigiri is spectacular." Our preferences are very diverse.

✧

The reason I don't make nigiri with it. Whitefish: *Madai Tai* north of Kanto doesn't swim in rough currents

Tai (sea bream) is superior among whitefish. If you compare delicious *tai* and delicious *hirame* (flounder), then the *tai* wins hands down. But I don't make nigiri with *tai*. That's because I just can't agree that *tai* swimming in a fish tank at Tsukiji Market tastes better than our best whitefish, which is *hirame* from Aomori.

When I was working in Osaka, I ate *tai* from Akashi for the first time in my life. For sure, I felt especially deeply moved because it was my first time. However, now, after over forty years, I still vividly remember what I tasted then.

Tai from Akashi had a different level of liveliness to its flesh compared to the *tai* that I was familiar with in Kanto. The color was different. The mouthfeel was different. The sweetness was different. The aroma was different. *Ah, I see. It can be this delicious.* It was just tasty beyond words.

In the Kyoto-Osaka area, there are people who are very particular about *tai*. That's because in that area, *uo* (fish) refers first and foremost to *madai* (red sea bream). For a long time, *tai* has remained the standard of deliciousness for fish there. That's how much they value the quality of whitefish.

If it's whitefish in Kansai, then in Tokyo it's *maguro* (tuna). To prove it, if you serve people from Kansai *shibi* (adult *kinkai hon maguro*), they won't find it too impressive. They might say, "*Setonai dai* (Seto Inland Sea sea bream) from Akashi or Naruto is more palatable."

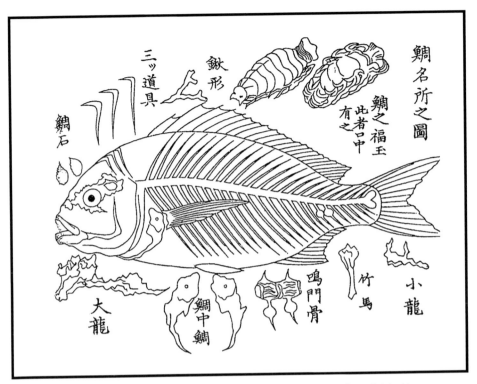

鯛名所之圖　三ッ道具　鍬形　鯛之福玉　此者口中有之　鯛石　大龍　鯛中鯛　鳴門骨　竹馬　小龍

Picture from the *tai* section of the book *Suizoku Shashin Setsu* (Pictorial View of Aquatic Animals) by Tatsuyuki Okukura, published at the end of the Edo period (1857). You can see two *naruto bone* (naruto bones) close to the end of the spine. (Archive of the National Diet Library)

To begin with, *tai* from Setonai and other *tai* differ in their very skeletal structure.

The skeleton of *odai* (big sea bream) from Setonai has two humps. The small bones that stretch from the spine to the belly are apparently called the hemal spine, and two of the small bones close to the tail are swollen at the base. I remember this well since I had trouble slicing it with my knife when I was working in Osaka.

When I saw this for the first time, I worried, thinking, "Did this one have some disease?" But the best-quality *akashi* always had humps, one after the other, when I sliced them.

I'm quoting a middle Edo-period book that a knowledgeable friend told me about, which says the following about these humps: "According to common wisdom, *tai* from the western sea crosses Naruto in Awa in spring and summer. Once it enters Ban (Harima) and Setsu (Settsu), [because of the extreme strong current] it grows humps in the big bone. Who knows if this is true" (Ryoan Terajima, *Wakan Sansai Zue*, Toyo Bunko).

A big bone is different from the spine, but what this doctor from the Edo period described is without question the humps that I remember of *akashi dai*. They must be like a callus grown from swimming in the swirling currents of the Seto Inland Sea. By the way, they call these humps *"naruto* (swirl) *bone* (bones)."

In fact, I believed until just recently that only *odai* from Setonai have the *naruto bone,* but a regular told me, *"Tai* from Ise Bay also have humps." Perhaps there are *tai* with humps in other seas.

In any case, *naruto bone* is a medal awarded to extraordinarily delicious *tai.* Come to think of it, they say the *tai* from Ise Bay is extraordinarily delicious, too.

But *tai* from north of the Kanto area don't grow *naruto bone* because they don't swim in rough currents. At least I have never seen it. This may be why I feel their flavor drops.

"Jiro doesn't make nigiri with *tai."*

Of course, our regulars know this, but first-time customers often ask for it. I'm left to wonder what kind of *tai* flavor they're expecting.

In this day and age, most *tai* is farmed. Good wild *madai* is eye-poppingly expensive and also very scarce. But sushi chefs who use farmed *tai* won't tell their customers each time, "This is farmed *tai."* They make nigiri with it, saying, "Yes, this is *tai."*

So I just don't know if the taste the customer is expecting is of the lively wild one or of the flabby and overly greasy farmed one.

It's the same for any fish, but I never want to use farmed seafood. They may look the same, but they have totally different flavors.

Also, as long as I'm in Tokyo, getting a stable supply of *kobu dai* (*tai* with bumps) is challenging. Therefore, when I receive an order for *tai*, I answer, "We don't have it. The only whitefish in winter is *hirame,"* and I have no intention of making nigiri with *tai* in the future, either.

Since the old days, at sushi restaurants in Tokyo, whitefish in the winter has meant *hirame*.

Chapter 2

Making Nigiri with *Hon Maguro*

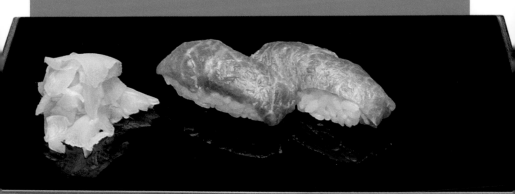

Map of *Hon Maguro* Migration around Japan

Hon maguro from the seas near Japan spawn in the area between Taiwan and Okinawa and swim northward along the coast of Japan. They eat plenty in the seas around Hokkaido rich in food, and the early ones start to swim south around October. There are a few that migrate toward the American west coast, crossing the Pacific Ocean while swimming northward. The locations on this map are the sources of *kinkai hon maguro* used at Sukiyabashi Jiro, and the dates note when the restaurant stocked them. By following the dates, the migration route of the *kinkai hon maguro* becomes clear.

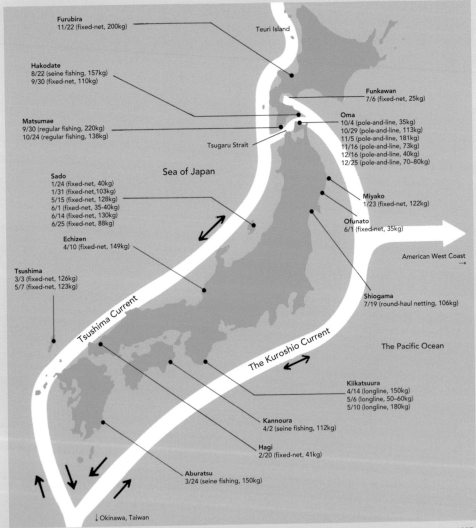

Furubira
11/22 (fixed-net, 200kg)

Teuri Island

Hakodate
8/22 (seine fishing, 157kg)
9/30 (fixed-net, 110kg)

Funkawan
7/6 (fixed-net, 25kg)

Matsumae
9/30 (regular fishing, 220kg)
10/24 (regular fishing, 138kg)

Oma
10/4 (pole-and-line, 35kg)
10/29 (pole-and-line, 113kg)
11/5 (pole-and-line, 181kg)
11/16 (pole-and-line, 73kg)
12/16 (pole-and-line, 40kg)
12/25 (pole-and-line, 70–80kg)

Tsugaru Strait

Sea of Japan

Sado
1/24 (fixed-net, 40kg)
1/31 (fixed-net, 103kg)
5/15 (fixed-net, 128kg)
6/1 (fixed-net, 35-40kg)
6/14 (fixed-net, 130kg)
6/25 (fixed-net, 88kg)

Miyako
1/23 (fixed-net, 122kg)

Ofunato
6/1 (fixed-net, 35kg)

Echizen
4/10 (fixed-net, 149kg)

Tsushima
3/3 (fixed-net, 126kg)
5/7 (fixed-net, 123kg)

American West Coast

Tsushima Current

Shiogama
7/19 (round-haul netting, 106kg)

The Kuroshio Current

The Pacific Ocean

Kiikatsuura
4/14 (longline, 150kg)
5/6 (longline, 50–60kg)
5/10 (longline, 180kg)

Kannoura
4/2 (seine fishing, 112kg)

Hagi
2/20 (fixed-net, 41kg)

Aburatsu
3/24 (seine fishing, 150kg)

↓ Okinawa, Taiwan

* The record is from May 1993 to Jan 1994 and Jun 1996 to Aug 1997.

Four Kinds of *Maguro* Nigiri

Otoro (*Jabara*/bellows belly), November, Oma

Out of *otoro*, "the bellows underbelly" is especially greasy. But its sinew is strong, so it's matured on ice. It takes skills to calculate when to use it. Rested for too long, its color, which is essential, starts to look dull, and moreover, the softened bellows belly's sinew stretches too much, which makes it hard to make nigiri with.

Otoro (*Shimofuri*/marbled flesh), April, Echizen

"Marbled flesh" is a rare nigiri-*dane*, but it's easier to make nigiri with than the bellows belly. The marbled flesh of a *maguro* that weighs under 150 kg has a light and refined taste like the *chutoro* of a larger *maguro*.

Chutoro July, Shiogama

Chutoro is the best liked. It offers a range from parts where you can enjoy the contrast of fat and lean meat to parts with strong fat.

Lean Meat, June, Sado

There are more orders for lean meat lately, more customers who appreciate the pleasant "smell of blood" and the umami brought about by its unique acidity. Lean meat that's fatty over autumn to winter is extra tasty.

99

Kami (upper) section

Kamashita (behind the gills). *Kami* has the most fat on it. The hollow part used to contain internal organs.

For the First Time in History:
A Complete Section of *Kinkai Hon Maguro!*

If you start under *kamashita* (behind the gills) of *kinkai hon maguro* and divide it in three—*kami* (upper part), *naka* (middle part), and *shimo* (lower part)—you can clearly see the fat, sinew, and coloring. When you make nigiri with it, the difference in the texture of flesh becomes even clearer.

Origin: Oma
Weight: 35 kilograms
Body length: 145 centimeters
Body height: 34 centimeters
Circumference: 93 centimeters
Fishing method: Pole-and-line fishing
Day caught: October 4th
Day photographed: October 7th

Maguro at the market is divided into four parts: upper, lower, belly, and back. So it's hard to tell the *otoro, chutoro,* and lean parts. Thus, we bought a whole fish and asked the broker Ishizuka at Tsukiji to cut it into round slices and then photographed them. It's an unprecedented project. Right after being caught, the color of the lean meat is similar to that of red muscle. But as time passes and it matures, it starts to brown and turn dark and dull. As *maguro* gets bigger, it gains fat not only on the belly side but also on the back side.

The sliced *kami* location

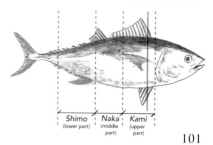

Shimo	Naka	Kami
(lower part)	(middle part)	(upper part)

101

❶ *Kami* (upper part), belly section,
otoro (*jabara*/bellows belly)

Underbelly close to the *kama* side. There's sinew
in a bellows pattern. When it matures, the sinew
softens to the point of melting in the mouth.

Kami (upper part), belly section,
otoro (*shimofuri*/marbled flesh)

The fat is marbled throughout, and there is no
sinew. The fatty content is somewhere between
the bellows belly of *otoro* and *chutoro*. It's a
rare item for which you get only one to three
saku (slab) out of a whole fish.

❷

❸

Kami (upper part), belly section, *chutoro*

There is only a little *chutoro* in the belly section.
It has moderate fat and is liked by everyone.

❹

Kami (upper part), belly section, lean meat

Lean meat can be found on top of the belly-
bone. The smell of blood gets stronger as
the lean meat gets closer to red muscle.

Kami (upper part), back section,
wakaremi

The back section of *kami* is found at the root of
the dorsal fin. It's a rare item for which you get
only one to two *saku* out of a whole fish. It's considered to be more premium than *chutoro*. It has
a smooth and unique flavor that's in between
chutoro and lean meat, but the drawback is that
its color changes quickly.

❺

Kami (upper part), back section, *chutoro*

Its fat is weaker than *chutoro's* belly section.
Especially with smaller *maguro*, the flesh
in this section is easy to split, so it's common to
use it for *tekka maki* (tuna roll).

❻

102

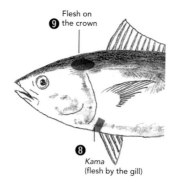

Flesh on
❾ the crown

❽
Kama
(flesh by the gill)

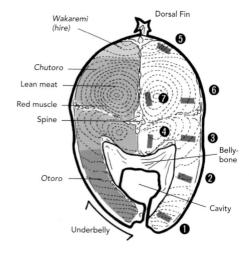

Dorsal Fin

Wakaremi
(hire)

❺

Chutoro

Lean meat

Red muscle

Spine

❼

❻

❹

❸

Belly-
bone

Otoro

❷

Cavity

Underbelly

❶

From *Kama* to *Naka:*
Making nigiri with eighteen parts

Kami (upper part), back section, lean meat

You get only three to four *saku* of lean meat
from the belly section, but six to seven from
the back section. Those from the back section
are better in aroma and acidity than those
from the belly section.

❼

❽

Kama (flesh by the gill)

Commonly called "the *otoro* of all *otoro*,"
but the sinew is tough, and it tends to
smell fishy. Not appropriate as nigiri-*dane*.

Flesh on the crown

The *maguro* brokers at the Tsukiji market
eat this part at home. It's the flesh that's
on the bones inside of the head. Softer
than the soft *kami chutoro* in the back
section, it has a creamy texture.

❾

The sliced *naka* location

Compared to *kami* (upper section), any part of *naka* has a lighter flavor. They say, "For the back, it's easier to use *naka*," because the sinew is softer than in *kami*.

Naka (middle) section

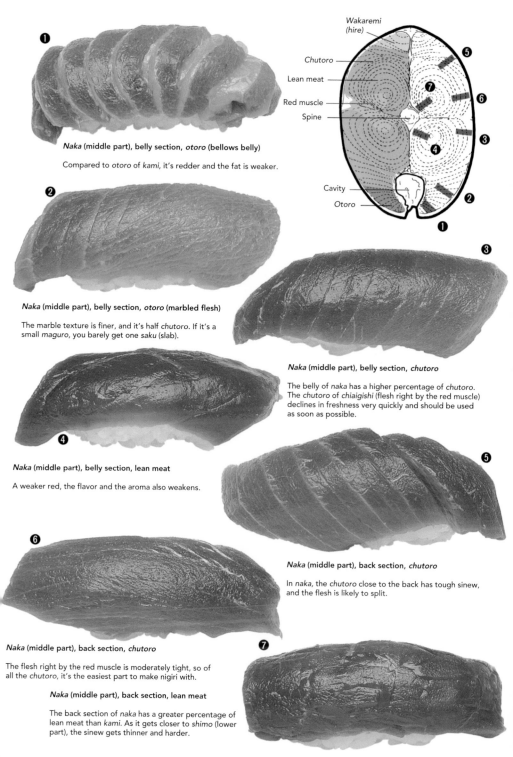

① Naka (middle part), belly section, otoro (bellows belly)

Compared to otoro of kami, it's redder and the fat is weaker.

② Naka (middle part), belly section, otoro (marbled flesh)

The marble texture is finer, and it's half chutoro. If it's a small maguro, you barely get one saku (slab).

③ Naka (middle part), belly section, chutoro

The belly of naka has a higher percentage of chutoro. The chutoro of chiaigishi (flesh right by the red muscle) declines in freshness very quickly and should be used as soon as possible.

④ Naka (middle part), belly section, lean meat

A weaker red, the flavor and the aroma also weakens.

⑤ Naka (middle part), back section, chutoro

In naka, the chutoro close to the back has tough sinew, and the flesh is likely to split.

⑥ Naka (middle part), back section, chutoro

The flesh right by the red muscle is moderately tight, so of all the chutoro, it's the easiest part to make nigiri with.

⑦ Naka (middle part), back section, lean meat

The back section of naka has a greater percentage of lean meat than kami. As it gets closer to shimo (lower part), the sinew gets thinner and harder.

Diagram labels:
Wakaremi (hire)
Chutoro
Lean meat
Red muscle
Spine
Cavity
Otoro

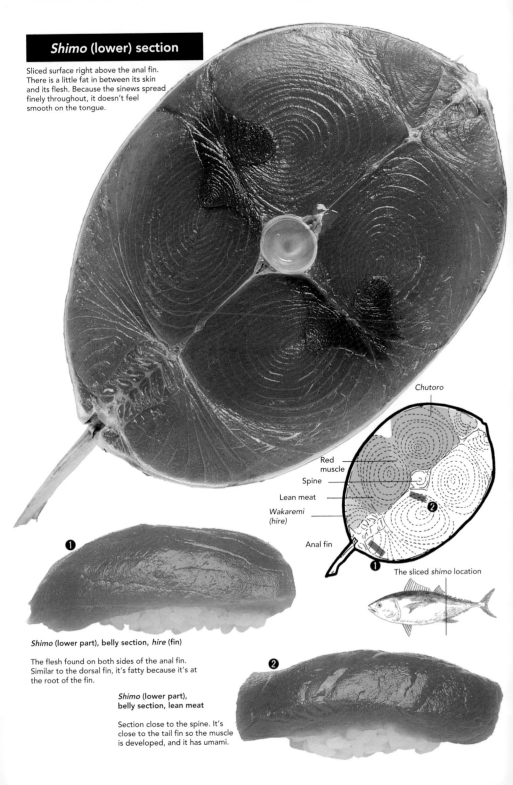

Shimo (lower) section

Sliced surface right above the anal fin. There is a little fat in between its skin and its flesh. Because the sinews spread finely throughout, it doesn't feel smooth on the tongue.

Chutoro

Red muscle

Spine

Lean meat

Wakaremi (hire)

Anal fin

❶

❷

The sliced *shimo* location

❶

Shimo (lower part), belly section, *hire* (fin)

The flesh found on both sides of the anal fin. Similar to the dorsal fin, it's fatty because it's at the root of the fin.

❷

Shimo (lower part), belly section, lean meat

Section close to the spine. It's close to the tail fin so the muscle is developed, and it has umami.

Maguro that they stock at Sukiyabashi Jiro is mainly *kami* (upper part) of the belly section (*harakami* No. 1), to make *otoro* nigiri, and a block from *naka* (middle part) of the back section, to make *chutoro* and lean meat nigiri. Section pictures that unfold from the following page show a total of thirteen pieces that include twelve pieces of *kami* of the belly section from over twelve months, and one piece of *naka* of the back section from October. Out of them, the belly section from February, November, and December and the back section from October are in their actual sizes. All nigiri are printed in their actual sizes as well.

• Data showed next to the section pictures
Origin: The locations of the catch and landing
Size: Weight of *maguro* including the head at the time
  of arrival
Part: *Harakami* is the belly section close to the head
Fishing method: Affects the quality of meat of *maguro*
Day photographed: Date purchased by Sukiyabashi Jiro
  (It's either the day of arrival at Tsukiji Chuo Market, or a
  couple of days after.)

• About *uwami* and *shitami* (top and bottom flesh)
When you place fish with its head facing left and its belly to you, we call the flesh on top *uwami* and the flesh on the bottom *shitami*. In the case of *maguro*, they determine which side of the flesh is the top or the bottom soon after it's caught by how it lay on a fishing boat. Because the flesh on top weighs down on the flesh on the bottom, causing it to fall apart, the flesh on top is considered to be of better quality. However, depending on where they were caught, sometimes *maguro* get flipped around, so the difference in quality is not always clear. Here, for the sake of convenience, we determined the flesh on top to be when the head is facing left.

• Looking at the photos
For the section photos of *maguro*, as a rule, the section viewed from the tail side is enlarged, and the section from the gill side is reduced.

Shoot period: From June 1996 to August 1997.
From November to December 1993.

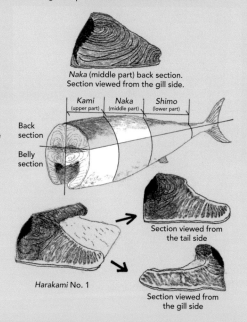

Naka (middle part) back section.
Section viewed from the gill side.

Harakami No. 1

Section viewed from
the tail side

Section viewed from
the gill side

107

Origin: Miyako
Size: 122 kilograms
Part: *Harakami* No. 1 *(shitami)*
Fishing method: Fixed-net fishing
Day photographed: January 23rd

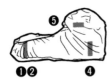

A much-awaited top-notch specimen that arrived right after New Year's in 1997. At a glance, you can tell, "This is good. It's fatty." Judging from the whiteness of the film on top of the belly bone, you can tell that it's a "young" (recently caught) *maguro*. It becomes good to eat after letting it mature over a bed of ice for four to five days.

Otoro (bellows belly)

The second *saku* (slab) from the underbelly. It has hard sinews, so it's used after resting for five days.

Otoro (bellows belly)

It's now good to eat. Compared to the nigiri on top, the sinews have softened.

108

Otoro (marbled flesh)

Kama-side section closer to *chutoro*.
The fat melts slowly on the tongue.

❸

Chutoro

❹ The second *saku* (slab) from the red muscle.
You can enjoy the flavor contrast between *toro*
to lean meat in this one piece.

❺

Lean Meat

It has plenty of fat on it. If you let it rest for four
to five days, the acidity and the aroma become
richer.

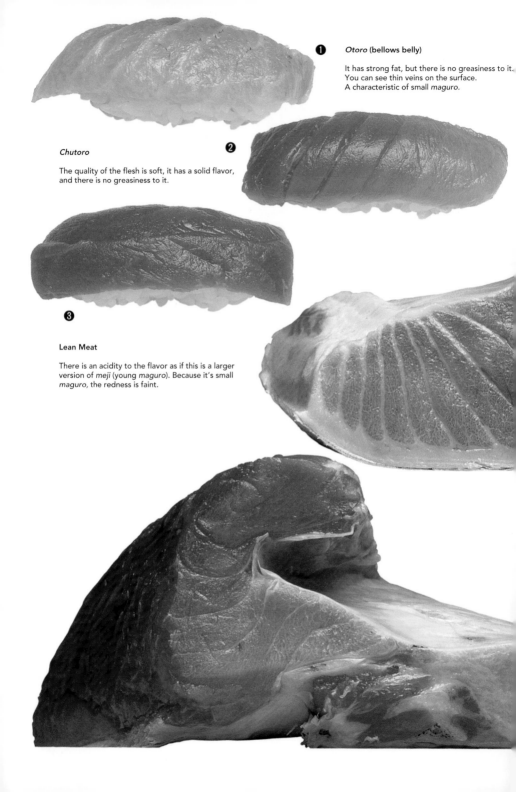

❶ *Otoro* (bellows belly)

It has strong fat, but there is no greasiness to it.
You can see thin veins on the surface.
A characteristic of small *maguro*.

Chutoro **❷**

The quality of the flesh is soft, it has a solid flavor,
and there is no greasiness to it.

❸

Lean Meat

There is an acidity to the flavor as if this is a larger
version of *meji* (young *maguro*). Because it's small
maguro, the redness is faint.

Origin: Hagi
Size: 41 kilograms
Part: *Harakami* No. 1 *(shitami)*
Fishing method: Fixed-net fishing
Day photographed: February 20th

Maguro that was in the middle of swimming southward in the Sea of Japan. It has a plain smooth flavor, because it's small. Three to four days had passed since it was caught. The day of the purchase and the following day was the best time to eat it. It wasn't taken care of well after it was caught, so the *maguro*'s body temperature didn't decrease, which resulted in the flesh burning a bit.

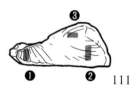

111

In a typical year, this is a time when most of the hon maguro are caught off Tosa, Kiikatsuura and Miyazaki, but in 1997, many came from the Sea of Japan. The form and the fattiness were not any worse than the one from Miyako in January. It was a bit young, so it became good to eat after three to four days.

①

Otoro (bellows belly)

The *saku* from the area close to the skin has a narrower gap in between sinews, so slice into it as if you're cutting off the sinews before making nigiri with it.

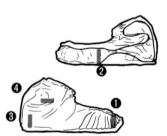

112

March

Origin: Tsushima
Size: 126 kilograms
Part: *Harakami* No. 1 *(uwami)*
Fishing method: Fixed-net fishing
Day photographed: March 3rd

Otoro (marbled flesh) ❷

The marbled patterns are more distinct with *maguro* that weigh over 100 kilograms.

Chutoro ❸

The second *saku* (slab) from the red muscle. The lean meat and the fatty part create a vignette of colors.

Lean Meat ❹

It's aromatic and has a slight sweetness and acidity. According to Jiro Ono, "It tastes much better than the 41-kg *maguro* that I used in February."

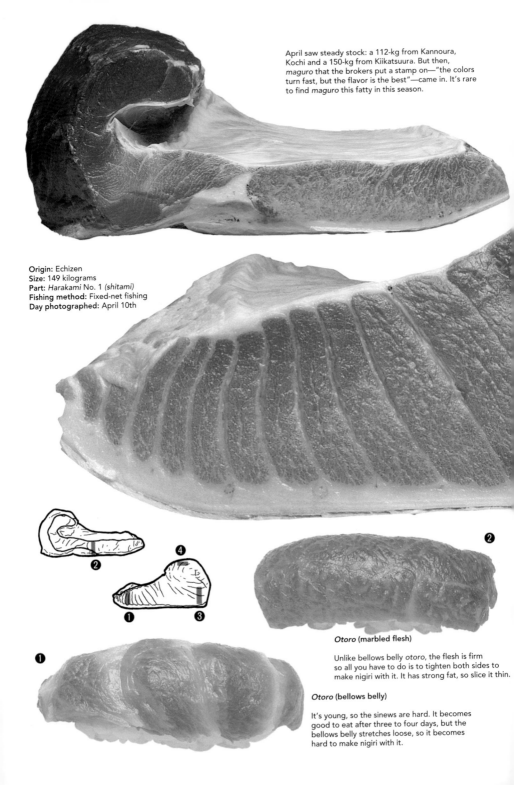

April saw steady stock: a 112-kg from Kannoura, Kochi and a 150-kg from Kiikatsuura. But then, *maguro* that the brokers put a stamp on—"the colors turn fast, but the flavor is the best"—came in. It's rare to find *maguro* this fatty in this season.

Origin: Echizen
Size: 149 kilograms
Part: *Harakami* No. 1 *(shitami)*
Fishing method: Fixed-net fishing
Day photographed: April 10th

Otoro (marbled flesh)

Unlike bellows belly *otoro*, the flesh is firm so all you have to do is to tighten both sides to make nigiri with it. It has strong fat, so slice it thin.

Otoro (bellows belly)

It's young, so the sinews are hard. It becomes good to eat after three to four days, but the bellows belly stretches loose, so it becomes hard to make nigiri with it.

Chutoro

Good quality *maguro* is distinct in its moist feel to the touch. The redness becomes stronger as it gets closer to red muscle.

3

4

Lean Meat

The one that arrived two days before couldn't be used because it was "bald *maguro*" with no umami at all. With this lean meat with fat, the colors may turn fast, but it has a great aroma and umami.

115

A lot of *maguro* is caught with *hikinawa* (seine fishing), and this *maguro* was the only one that was caught with *teichiami* (fixed-net fishing). It has the same origin as the *maguro* from March (page 113), and the shape is almost identical. But it doesn't have too much fat on it, so the lean meat is prominent. Overall, it tasted young like *meji* (young *maguro*).

❶

❷

Otoro (marbled flesh)

It has become good to eat. The fat spreads as soon as you put it in your mouth.

Otoro (bellows belly)

The stamina of *maguro* caught in seas around Japan tends to decline in May, but this one has a decent fat layer. Its colors may fade quickly because it wasn't handled right subsequent to its capture.

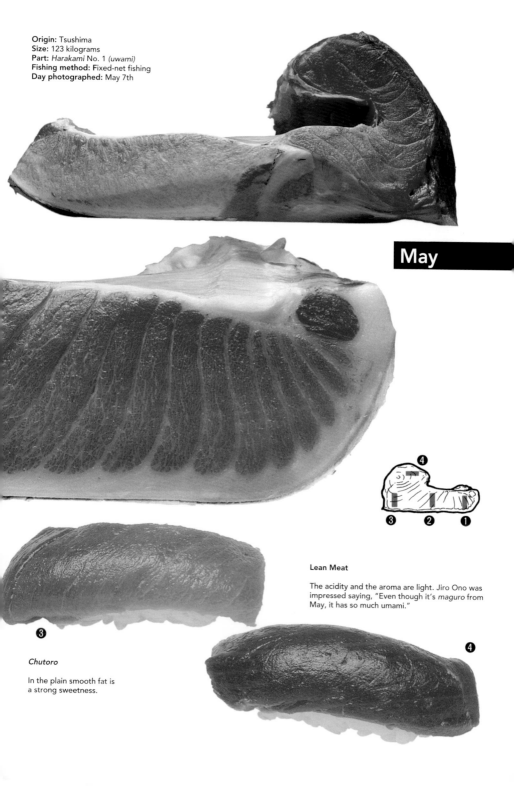

Origin: Tsushima
Size: 123 kilograms
Part: *Harakami* No. 1 *(uwami)*
Fishing method: Fixed-net fishing
Day photographed: May 7th

May

Lean Meat

The acidity and the aroma are light. Jiro Ono was impressed saying, "Even though it's *maguro* from May, it has so much umami."

Chutoro

In the plain smooth fat is a strong sweetness.

Origin: Sado
Size: 130 kilograms
Part: *Harakami* No. 1 *(shitami)*
Fishing method: Fixed-net fishing
Day photographed: June 14th

In June, *chubo* (medium-sized *maguro*) arrives from Sanin. And mixed with large-sized *maguro* that were caught with *makiami* (round-haul netting) from off Choshi and Sanriku, the *"teichiami" (maguro* caught with fixed-net fishing) comes in from Sado. Still skinny, it was on its way north to Hokkaido, chasing after food. Out of seven *kinkai maguro* that were auctioned at Tsukiji Market that day, this one was evaluated to be the best.

Otoro (bellows belly)

Despite its large size, the belly flesh is thin, and the fat is weak. It tastes plain.

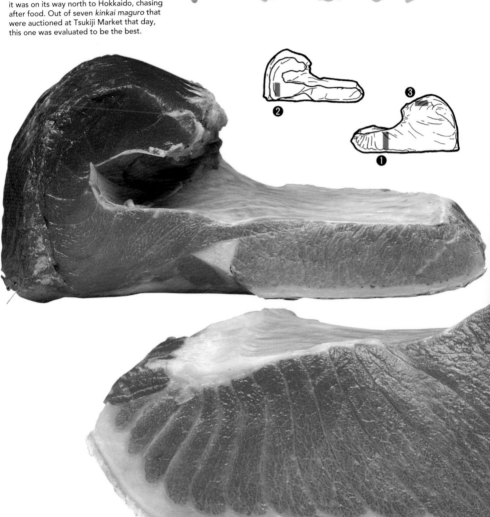

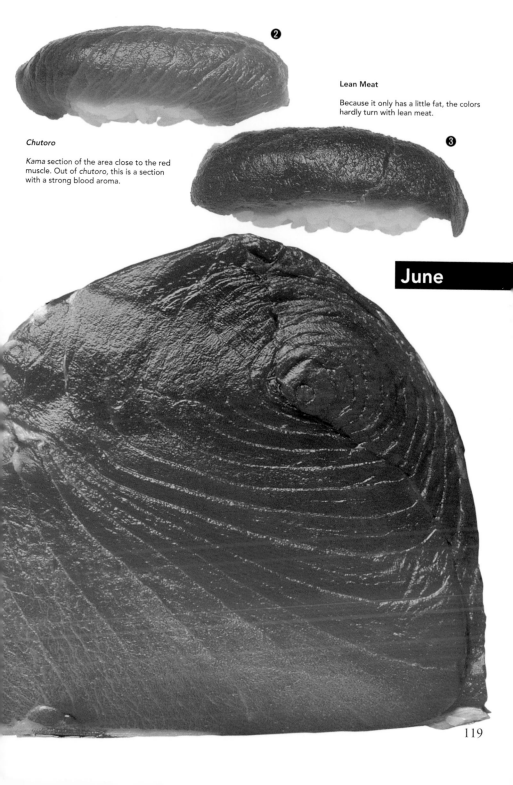

Chutoro

Kama section of the area close to the red muscle. Out of *chutoro*, this is a section with a strong blood aroma.

Lean Meat

Because it only has a little fat, the colors hardly turn with lean meat.

June

119

Chutoro

This nigiri is from a section next to the clavicle, which bites into the flesh, at the border of *otoro* and *chutoro* on the *kama* side. Because it's summer *maguro*, it's skinny and has less fat.

❷

Otoro (in between bellows belly and marbled flesh)

Because it doesn't have strong fat, it's not greasy and has plenty of umami.

❶

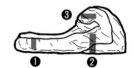

Origin: Shiogama
Size: 106 kilograms
Part: *Harakami* No. 1 *(uwami)*
Fishing method: Round-haul netting
Day photographed: July 19th

There aren't too many good quality *hon maguro* in the summertime. Even when brokers win bids thinking they were good *maguro*, there are times when after it's opened it's all black inside and can't be used. This one from Shiogama a day or two after the catch is fatty for summer *maguro*. With *maguro* in the summertime, if you let it rest for two or three more days, the umami will increase, but the colors fade quickly, so it's hard to determine the timing.

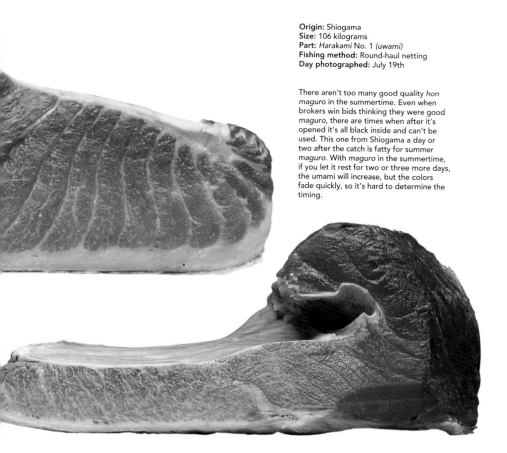

Lean Meat

It's moist and smooth. When you let it rest, its flavor deepens, but it doesn't make as much of a difference as with *otoro*. The color fading is the bigger issue.

121

1

Otoro (marbled flesh)

It's fatty like an *oma* from the beginning of autumn. At this level, even if you let it rest until it's good to eat, you don't have to worry about the colors fading.

Otoro (bellows belly)

From the *kama* side of an underbelly *saku* (slab). Compared to bellows belly *otoro* on the tail side, it has strong and hard sinews. Typically, you carefully get rid of them after cutting out the *saku*.

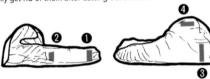

2

Although the ones from Oma and Matsumae that came in at the beginning of August looked nice and red, they were just okay fattiness-wise. After July 15th, a bountiful twenty-two *maguro* came in from Shiogama and Kesennuma. But they were all too skinny. Out of the ten *maguro* from Hokkaido in the next batch, this one from Hakodate was of the best quality. Even the broker who won the bid was surprised, saying, "This is superlative summer *maguro*. I haven't seen one with a belly this thick in recent years."

122

Chutoro

The *saku* (slab) next to red muscle. *Tane* has been sliced on the long side, but instead of chopping off the excess, fold in while making nigiri. The flavor of *chutoro* is only complete when the range from lean to fatty is featured.

❸

❹

Lean Meat

From *saku* (slab) next to bone, sliced from the tail side. Unlike typical summer *maguro* lean meat, you can clearly see that it's fatty.

August

Origin: Hakodate
Size: 157 kilograms
Part: *Harakami* No. 1 *(shitami)*
Fishing method: Seine fishing
Day photographed: August 22nd

Otoro (bellows belly)

When you cut into the *tane*, a knife hits hard on the sinews of *maguro* imported from overseas. However, a knife can move smoothly through *kinkai maguro*.

Otoro (marbled flesh)

You can only get two or three "*shimofuri* (marbled)" *saku* (slabs) from this block. If you let it rest for two days, the flavor deepens enough to make you purr.

Origin: Hakodate
Size: 110 kilograms
Part: *Harakami* No. 1 *(uwami)*
Fishing method: Fixed-net fishing
Day photographed: September 30th

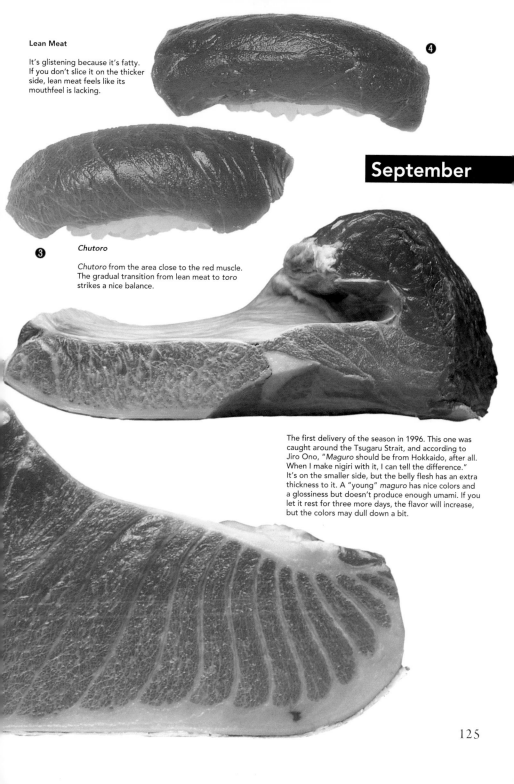

Lean Meat

It's glistening because it's fatty. If you don't slice it on the thicker side, lean meat feels like its mouthfeel is lacking.

❹

❸ *Chutoro*

Chutoro from the area close to the red muscle. The gradual transition from lean meat to *toro* strikes a nice balance.

The first delivery of the season in 1996. This one was caught around the Tsugaru Strait, and according to Jiro Ono, "*Maguro* should be from Hokkaido, after all. When I make nigiri with it, I can tell the difference." It's on the smaller side, but the belly flesh has an extra thickness to it. A "young" *maguro* has nice colors and a glossiness but doesn't produce enough umami. If you let it rest for three more days, the flavor will increase, but the colors may dull down a bit.

125

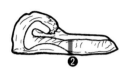
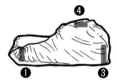

Origin: Matsumae
Size: 138 kilograms
Part: *Harakami* No. 1 *(shitami)*
Fishing method: Regular fishing
Day photographed: October 24th

According to Jiro Ono, "When caught with *ipponzuri* (pole-and-line fishing), *tsuri* (fishing) or *ami* (net), the flesh quality of *maguro* is plain and smooth. On the other hand, ones caught with *nawa* (rope, or a long line with many hooks) have too strong fat and their burnt colors bother me as well." This *maguro* from Matsumae has vivid colors. The quality of flesh was moist and it also had good fattiness.

Otoro (bellows belly)

Because it's too young, the sinews are hard. If you slice it thick, you can't chew it off. Let it rest and mature for three to four days.

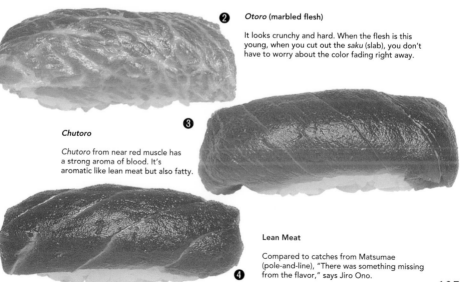

② *Otoro* (marbled flesh)

It looks crunchy and hard. When the flesh is this young, when you cut out the *saku* (slab), you don't have to worry about the color fading right away.

③ Chutoro

Chutoro from near red muscle has a strong aroma of blood. It's aromatic like lean meat but also fatty.

④ Lean Meat

Compared to catches from Matsumae (pole-and-line), "There was something missing from the flavor," says Jiro Ono.

127

November

Origin: Furubira
Size: 200 kilograms
Part: *Harakami* No. 1 *(shitami)*
Fishing method: Fixed-net fishing
Day photographed: November 22nd

Lately, there are fewer large *kinkai maguro* that weigh over 200 kilograms. This one was caught off the coast of Shakotan Peninsula, and the belly part is plump with a nice fatty layer. When it gets this big, the sinew starts to appear clearly in the *kama* section too. After letting it rest for a week, it's good to eat starting with the exposed parts.

* This spread folds out to three pages.
Enjoy it in the actual size, in all its grandeur.

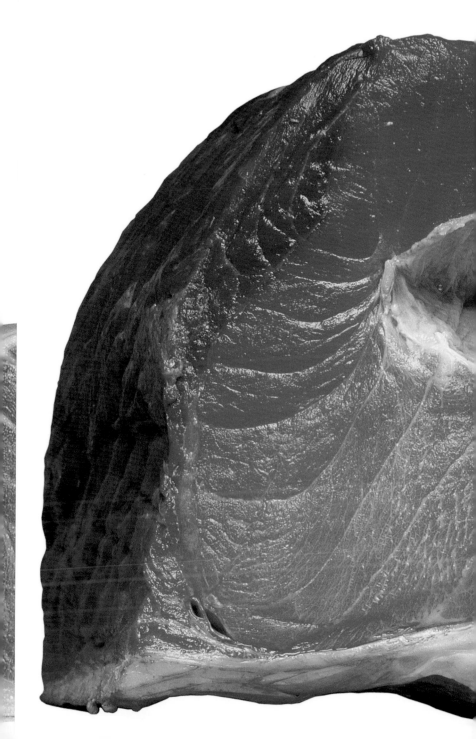

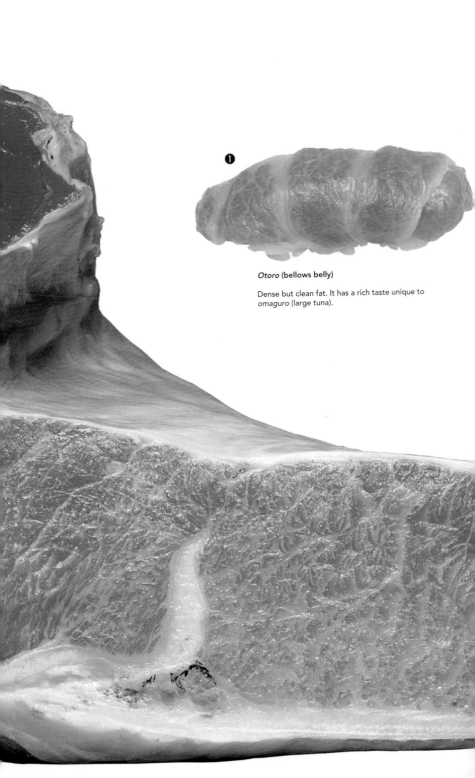

❶

Otoro (bellows belly)

Dense but clean fat. It has a rich taste unique to *omaguro* (large tuna).

Chutoro

While it's a *chutoro* with evenly spread fat,
out of a large block you get only three to
four *saku* (slabs).

Lean Meat

It loses its glossiness after maturing, but softens
while maintaining a firm texture.

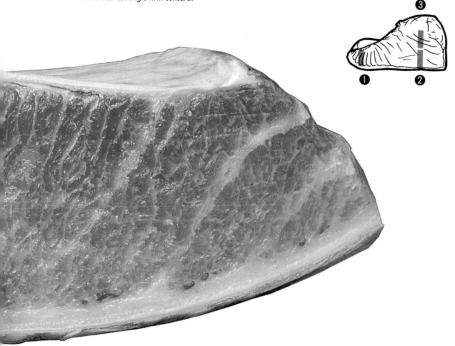

Origin: Oma
Size: 40 kilograms
Part: *Harakami* No. 1 *(uwami)*
Fishing method: Pole-and-line fishing
Day photographed: December 16th

Maguro from Oma keeps rising in reputation. The quality is good, and it's taken care of skillfully, so they can charge a high price as soon as it's labeled an *oma*. Although small, this one was the best in recent years. No *hon maguro* has appeared to surpass this "40-kg *oma*" yet.

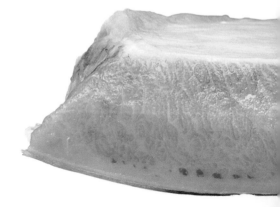

Otoro (bellows belly)

❶

Because it's a small *maguro*, the gaps between sinews are narrow. But there is no greasiness to the flesh.

Chutoro

Light flavor gradation.

❷

❸

Lean Meat

Plenty of aroma and sweetness, and a depth to the flavor.

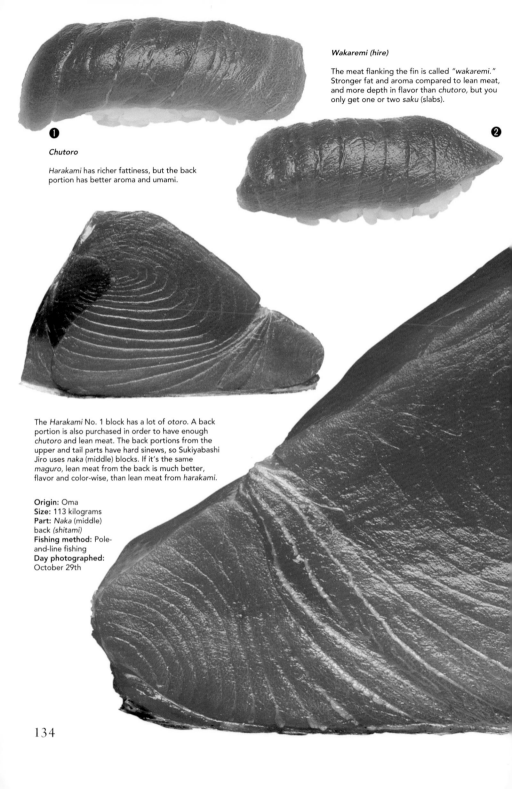

Wakaremi (hire)

The meat flanking the fin is called "*wakaremi.*" Stronger fat and aroma compared to lean meat, and more depth in flavor than *chutoro*, but you only get one or two *saku* (slabs).

①

②

Chutoro

Harakami has richer fattiness, but the back portion has better aroma and umami.

The *Harakami* No. 1 block has a lot of *otoro*. A back portion is also purchased in order to have enough *chutoro* and lean meat. The back portions from the upper and tail parts have hard sinews, so Sukiyabashi Jiro uses *naka* (middle) blocks. If it's the same *maguro*, lean meat from the back is much better, flavor and color-wise, than lean meat from *harakami*.

Origin: Oma
Size: 113 kilograms
Part: *Naka* (middle) back *(shitami)*
Fishing method: Pole-and-line fishing
Day photographed: October 29th

Lean Meat

Plenty of aroma and umami.
With a little more time, the flavor will deepen.

❸

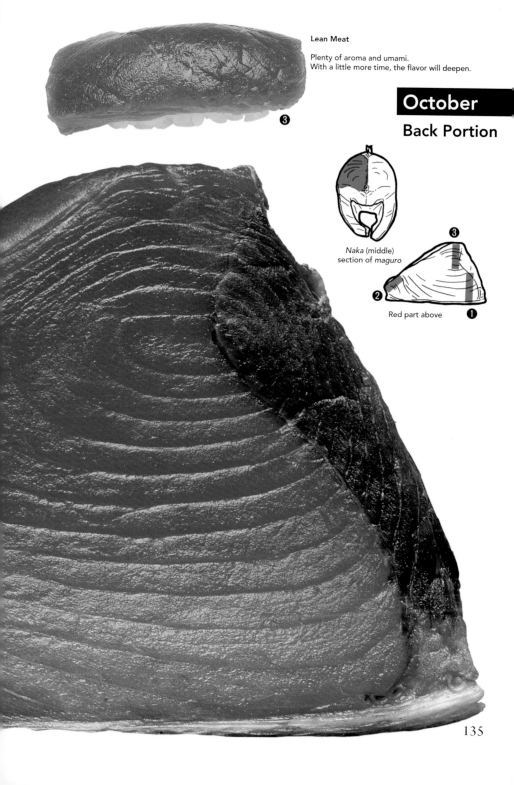

Naka (middle)
section of *maguro*

❸

❷

❶

Red part above

135

Getting *saku* out of *maguro*

Insert the knife in between the red muscle and lean meat.

Using the collarbone on the *kama* side as a guide, divide and slice apart *otoro* and *chutoro*.

Carve out the red muscle as if you're peeling it.

From the left: lean meat, *chutoro*, and *otoro*. For *harakami* no. 1 from a 180-kg *maguro*, the ratio is 2:3:4.

Insert the knife parallel to the cutting board and according to the thickness of the bellows part.

Slice apart one *saku* of marbled *otoro*. The thickness should be 2.5 cm (an inch).

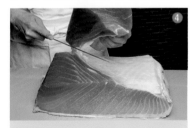

Separate the lean meat.

Slice apart one *saku* of bellows belly on the underbelly side. The white fat right by the skin has a smell, so remove and discard.

Slice apart one *saku* of *chutoro* by the red muscle. It has a vivid contrast ranging from lean meat to *toro*.

Slice off the membrane of the abdominal cavity that remains on the block of lean meat.

Slice the first *saku* of lean meat as if you're cutting off the sinews vertically.

From the left: lean meat, *chutoro*, marbled *otoro*, and bellows belly *otoro*.

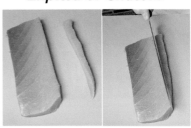

(pencil)
Enpitsu of *Chutoro*

If the *saku* (slab) of *chutoro* is wide, then adjust it to the size of nigiri by chopping off the fatty side closer to the skin. With *chutoro* you want to be enjoying the whole range from lean to fatty. The cut-off *enpitsu* (pencil) is also sliced and used to make nigiri. It's "the King of *Chutoro*" that you only get in very small portions.

Chijire of *Maguro*
(crimping of tuna)

Maguro caught by "the evening net" in Sado arrives at Tsukiji Market the following morning. Slicing into maguro that hasn't yet gone into rigor mortis leaves a dimple-like dent on the surface. If you force a *saku* (slab) out of such *maguro*, the live flesh crimps and it'll be hard to slice. This is called *chijire*. If you let it rest in a bed of ice, the *chijire* disappears and the umami comes forth.

137

Zuke of Maguro
(soy sauce-marinated tuna)

Zuke of maguro, March, Aburatsu

Adding umami by marinating *maguro* that has started to look dull in *nikiri* (thin and sweet glaze) originated in the past. The refreshing sanguine aroma inherent in lean meat disappears, but the richness unique to *zuke* comes forth. Sukiyabashi Jiro marinates enough for three to four people. Reservation required.

① A 150 kg from Aburatsu—get a *saku* (slab) out of the *naka* back portion. The first *saku* next to the edge is too soft and not the best for *zuke*.

② Run the knife through as if you're cutting off the sinews vertically.

③ Slice off a slab at the regular thickness for lean meat.

④ The part doesn't determine how the *saku* is scored, but depending on the quality, how much it marinates differs. The richer the fat, the less absorbent.

⑤ Marinate the *maguro saku* (slab) in *nikiri* (cooled-down reduction sauce of sake and soy sauce).

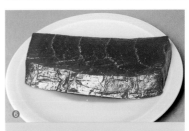

⑥ Marinate it at room temperature for half an hour, and it's done.

⑦ Slice as thick as normal lean meat. If the *nikiri* hasn't soaked in enough, then after making nigiri with it, brush some on the middle.

MAKING NIGIRI WITH
HON MAGURO

"I'll tell you what the pops of a sushi restaurant who
insists on ones from nearby seas really thinks."

The appeal of *kinkai hon maguro* (bluefin tuna from "near" or Japanese seas),
a.k.a. *shibi* (adult tuna), is the sweet smell of its blood. And the beautiful colors of the
nigiri. But *hon maguro* (bluefin tuna), especially its *otoro* (fatty tuna), is expensive.
It's expensive, but sushi chefs still make nigiri with it, prepared to be in the red.
This is a story of pride about "the King of Nigiri."

Ever since *Edomae*-style sushi was created, "the *Yokozuna* (sumo wrestling
champion) of Nigiri" has been *kohada* (gizzard shad) and "the *Yokozuna* of
Makimono (roll)" *kanpyo* (dried gourd). And *shibi* (adult bluefin tuna), good
to make nigiri with and good to roll, is surely worthy to be called "the King
of Sushi."

As *shibi* gets more delicious, making nigiri with it feels different to the touch, especially during the season when it gets extra fatty, from late autumn to winter.

And when you bite into it, a subtle sweet and sour aroma wafts through the nose, and an unobtrusive, light sweetness and bitterness spread in the mouth. This precisely is the aroma and flavor of the blood of red-fleshed fish that swim around the vast ocean. At a glance, it looks shiny with its fat spread evenly, but it feels quite greasy. Even the sinew that's supposed to be hard melts once it touches the tongue.

I think we can say that the appeal of *kinkai hon maguro* is the refreshing aroma and flavor of its blood. But since they're ever so subtle, the only time you clearly feel them is the moment you put it in your mouth, and then as you chew, you can't identify it any longer.

Not only for *maguro* but also for other *neta*, you can discern the subtle differences in aroma by pushing the *neta* onto your palate the moment you put it in your mouth. Ascertain the aroma by letting the smell travel up through the nose. You can't tell just with your tongue; there are different parts of the taste buds that are sensitive to sweetness, sourness, saltiness, bitterness, and spiciness, so don't taste with your tongue but with your nose. This technique is not taught by anyone but is something you have to learn naturally as a chef.

Having said that, with *maguro* the color is essential. The vivid shine, as if it's dripping, does much to stimulate your appetite. The glossy and deep-colored lean meat. The little fatty droplets that shine on the *neta*'s surface with *chutoro* (medium-fatty tuna) and *otoro* (fatty tuna). The white *shari* (vinegared rice) foundation. Facing the beautiful contrast of red and white and thinking "oh, it looks so good" deepens your experience of the flavor.

For a sushi restaurant master, bringing these colors and umami to life and making them coexist is a chance to show off.

Young *maguro* that has just been caught may have a nice coloring, but the flesh still feels crisp, and its sinew is too hard to chew. Its blood has a fishy smell that's far from a nice aroma.

So if a *maguro* you buy is "young" (just caught), you have to wait for it to mature on ice. Once it's matured, the sharp and fishy smell turns into a

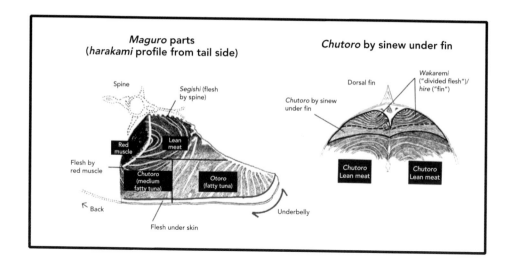

Maguro parts
(*harakami* profile from tail side)

Chutoro by sinew under fin

Spine

Segishi (flesh by spine)

Chutoro by sinew under fin

Dorsal fin

Wakaremi ("divided flesh")/ *hire* ("fin")

Red muscle

Lean meat

Flesh by red muscle

Chutoro (medium fatty tuna)

Otoro (fatty tuna)

Chutoro Lean meat

Chutoro Lean meat

Back

Flesh under skin

Underbelly

refreshing aroma. The fat spreads gently around the sinews of the *otoro*, and they soften. Its flavor and aroma reach their peak after it matures, and the fresh red meat starts to turn dark and dull. It's true, especially for the *otoro* and *chutoro* portions. Much like beef, the stage before it starts to oxidize is when the flavor deepens; there are many *maguro* that challenge me to decide between the delicious flavor and aroma, on the one hand, and the beautiful appetite-whetting hues on the other.

"If you want to eat delicious things, then become a regular."

What I especially like is a part called the marbled *harakami* that melts in the mouth like light snow. I always gaze with fascination at the *kanoko* (traditional Japanese dotted pattern), which looks like premium beef loin. The bellows underbelly is delicious beyond compare. *Kamashita* (the part under the gills) that has strong sinew is called "the *otoro* of *otoro*," but because it has a strong fishy smell, people's preferences may be divided.

The most delicious part of *chutoro* is said to be the *hire*, the divided flesh right by the dorsal fin. I agree. It has no sinew, and its fat is smooth and light, and there is no greasiness to it. The drawback is the limited quantity. You only get one or two slabs off the back portion, so it's not something we can have all the time. It's "the Phantom *Chutoro*" so to speak.

In fact, there is another gem that surpasses "the Phantom *Chutoro*."

When I slice into *wakaremi* (divided flesh), there is sinew, and in between, there is a tiny amount of flesh. In general, the flesh around bones or sinew is delicious, but even amongst them, this one tastes extraordinary. However, this particular sinew is tough and very difficult to remove.

This is why we make *tekka maki* (tuna roll) with it—because once it's diced, you can't feel the texture of the sinew. But it's far more delicious to remove the *wakaremi* and make nigiri with it. I compared them by eating it both ways and came to this conclusion, so I work on it, although it takes a lot of effort.

If there is even a little bit of sinew, you can feel it in your mouth. When I painstakingly try to remove it with a younger chef, even with two of us it takes at least half an hour. So we calculate the time and start to work on it a little bit after 6 p.m., when it's not so busy, then start to make nigiri with it for the guests who arrive around 7 p.m. This is a part whose color changes drastically, so after an hour or so, it starts to darken.

The parts under the fin that are removed vary in richness of flavor from those of *chutoro*, which is closer to lean meat, to those of *otoro*, which is very fatty. So I put them in the refrigerator while dividing the parts, remembering "the one with the stronger flavor is for this guest" and "the one with the lighter flavor is for that guest." This is a rare item from which I can make only fifteen to sixteen pieces of nigiri. It's not a *neta* that I can always serve, so I only make this nigiri if I really want a guest to taste it. It's a *chutoro* "specially tailored to regulars," if you will.

There are other *neta* that I don't serve unless you're a regular.

When I cut and remove *saku* (slabs) from a fatty, plump *maguro*, the *chutoro saku* always end up wide. When I slice them into nigiri-*dane* to match the size of *shari* (vinegared rice), I have to cut off the excess. In this case, I thinly slice off the fatty part right by the skin, not the lean meat. If I don't leave the lean meat, I can't bring out the gradation of flavors from plain to rich, which is the true pleasure of *chutoro*.

The part I remove is about two to three centimeters tall and wide and looks like a thick and long square pencil. It has soft fat spread all around, so when you put the *neta* on your tongue, it melts without any resistance and becomes one with the *shari*. Only umami remains in the mouth.

So my satisfied regulars who like *chutoro* always say without exception: "This is the king of *chutoro*."

When I share this kind of thing, some people may get angry, saying, "What the heck, you only give special treatment to your regulars."

That's not the case. Since I want my guests to enjoy eating nigiri, I can't just casually serve everything without knowing their preferences.

Because even if I made scarce *shimofuri* (marbled flesh) or *enpitsu* (the pencil-shaped cut described previously) nigiri, first-time customers might prefer plain lean meat. Meanwhile, I know for sure that my regulars, who arrive an hour later, get super happy when I serve them these. So it's human nature to say, I'll keep it for them. As the master of a sushi restaurant.

Also *toro*, compared to other attractions such as *kohada* (gizzard shad), *saba* (mackerel), and *anago* (conger eel), is far more expensive, so unless they order it, I can't just go ahead and make it.

This is why I tell my younger guys, "If you want to eat delicious things, then become a regular." It's okay until you find your favorite restaurant, but if you always keep searching for new restaurants—"I tried ten restaurants out of twenty on the restaurant guide, now I'll go visit the remaining ten"—you'll never be able to eat a rare *neta* like *chutoro* on the sinew under the fin. Then you're missing out.

The best time to encounter supreme *shibi* is the middle of autumn. Usually, the last good catch of *shibi* in Hokkaido or Aomori comes in late November to early December, and in December *maguro* start to swim south toward the Pacific Ocean and the Sea of Japan off the mainland.

Thus, the main fishing location from January to April is off the coasts of Kyushu and Shikoku. *Maguro* caught in these areas is transported to Kiikatsuura or Aburatsu (Miyazaki), but I can't find the kind that I like, and there

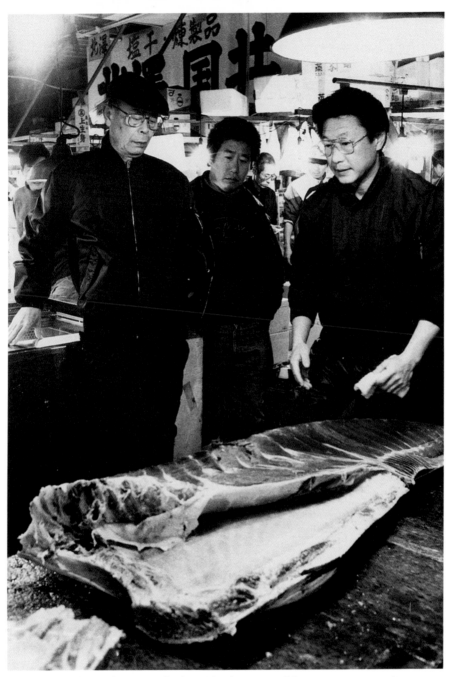

He doesn't buy every day but visits the *maguro* fishmonger every morning.
Pictured is an air-transported *maguro*. His eyes are stern as he tries to evaluate the
fatty content and the flesh quality.

are days that I'm at my wits' end. Some people may disagree, but I think it may be because they catch them with *haenawa* (longline fishing gear).

Around early autumn, when they start to recover from the spawning season in April to May, all the fat is gone, to the point that it feels cruel. I respectfully avoid these sleek skin-and-bone *shibi*. Conveniently, *chubo* (mid-sized *shibi*) that start to get caught in fixed nets off the coast of Sanin in late spring taste decent, so for a while, they decorate our *neta* box. Good-quality ones are also caught in Sado and Ofunato.

August is the worst. The *shibi* does retain its red coloring, but it's flavor-less like when you chew on *konnyaku* (yam cake). There is no fat. There is no richness to it. Or, *maguro* that have turned a dull color due to the heat line up at the market. But I am somewhat at ease since there are many off days during August. And by the time September comes around, the flavor starts to return to *shibi,* and the best season arrives shortly.

It's a delightful phenomenon that people are starting to prefer lean meat

Lately, there are more orders for lean meat. Occasionally there are orders for *zuke* (marinated), made after dipping it in *nikiri shoyu* (a thin and sweet soy sauce glaze). But if they said "two *kan* (pieces) of *zuke*" on the spot, they won't be delicious *zuke*.

If I lightly score the nigiri-*dane*, it gets marinated after just five minutes or so. However, I marinate it as a *saku* (slab) because the inherent aroma of *maguro* would disappear if the *nikiri* flavor penetrated all the way. If I receive a reservation—"I'd like to order *zuke* and will arrive at such and such an hour," then I observe the lean meat *saku*'s thickness and quality. And then I count backwards from the guest's arrival and marinate it for twenty to thirty minutes.

Of course, if it's delicious lean meat, then I think it's best to make nigiri with it as is to bring out the inherent aroma of *maguro*. It's not necessary to marinate it in *nikiri*.

After all, it's a delightful phenomenon that people are starting to prefer lean meat. There were close to no guests who ordered lean meat à la carte seven to eight years ago.

Sixty percent of the back flesh is lean meat, and the other forty percent is *chutoro*. So *chutoro* went quickly and the lean meat remained. It used to be, "So…what shall we do with this mountain of lean meat?" We couldn't possibly have it in the kitchen day and night, day in and day out, just because it was left over.

As a desperate measure, we used to deliver *tekka don* (tuna bowls) for lunch. We could easily accommodate huge orders—"Please bring fifty bowls right away"—because there was more than a great deal of lean meat. We just had to make the *shari*.

As someone who went through such trouble, I have to be very deeply grateful for food critics who passionately preached, "The essence of *maguro* lies in the lean meat. Sushi lovers, eat your lean meat." They increased the number of people who like lean meat. I sincerely think so.

If you want to know why customers back then ate so much *toro*, it's because it wasn't super expensive like it is now. They say, "People only started to prefer *toro* after the war and had lean meat in the old days," but that's towards the end of the shogunate or the Meiji period; by Taisho and Showa (the entre-guerre years), *chutoro* was eaten very often.

Kyobashi's master chef once told me a story. When he was younger, long before World War II, it was challenging for him to slice the bellows belly of *otoro* because it was sinewy. Yet a beginner could slice *chutoro* and lean meat without difficulty, so even for delivery *nami sushi* (the regular-grade assortment), he used *chutoro* that cut like *yokan* (sweet jellied azuki-bean paste). When his master found out, he was severely scolded: "You bastard! Why don't you use the cheap *otoro*?" Even back then, *chutoro* was a premium *neta* for customers who ordered à la carte.

Also, *shibi* was never a fish that was so expensive that we had to hold it reverently over our heads. According to my memory, in 1955, it cost two to three thousand yen per *kanme*, or five to eight hundred yen per kilo. *Kuruma ebi* (prawn) or *aka gai* (surf clam) was far more expensive. *Shibi* was a very familiar, common *neta*. So customers didn't make a fuss chanting, "*Hon maguro, hon maguro.*"

On top of that, when summer came, *shibi* was half-priced. Back then, they used to migrate off Mt. Kinka (at the tip of the Oshika Peninsula in Miyagi Prefecture) to the waters near Choshi, so *Edomae*-style *maguro* sushi was from Mt. Kinka and Choshi, but *shibi* in the summertime was so sleek that you couldn't eat it. People back then didn't even bother.

So what the fishermen targeted was the medium-sized *chubo*. When it grew to a certain point, it had a decent fatty layer. Plus, we were able to get ahold of endless amounts of *harakami* (the belly portion closest to the gills), which tasted good.

They didn't have to use the sinewy tail part like we do nowadays; it's like a joke when I come to think of it.

This is why Kyobashi's master chef used to say, "Sell *maguro* at the same price throughout the year. We might not make a profit during winter, but it's half-priced during the summer. It comes out even over the course of the year." However, it's the other way around now. Lately, in the summertime, the price goes up, not down. Coming out even profit-wise is a pipe dream.

It makes sense. They used to treat *shibi* as "the King of Nigiri" only in Tokyo, so there was a balance between demand and supply.

When I was working as a master-for-hire at a sushi restaurant in Osaka, the fish markets in the Kyoto-Osaka area didn't sell *hon maguro*. They had delicious whitefish, so the red meat *maguro* was considered to be a low-grade fish.

I used to reluctantly fly in *harakami* from Tsukiji, but it became pricey because of the transportation fee. So there were many customers who didn't order it, saying, "I don't like *maguro* because it's so expensive." Now, even in Osaka, *maguro* has become "the King of Nigiri."

It's not only Osaka. All the first-class sushi restaurants around the country compete to make nigiri with *hon maguro*, so even if fishermen do catch the same amount in seas near Japan, no wonder they don't have enough.

Moreover, the number of *shibi* is declining. We only got one in ten years from off Mt. Kinka, once considered the supreme kind by sushi restaurants in Tokyo. And actually that was bad quality. They say perhaps it's because they're caught in Hokkaido or the Strait of Tsugaru in the autumn before *shibi* start to migrate. Or that they don't get caught in fixed nets in Yoichi (Sea of Japan, Hokkaido) because too many are caught in early summer off the Sanin coast. Or that the currents have changed. There are people who try to come up with various reasons, but there are fewer *shibi* in the seas around Japan. What's more, the ones that make your heart skip a beat are getting rarer and rarer.

There is a reason I don't like *'nawa*

The best *chubo* that I made nigiri with was from Oma on the Strait of Tsugaru and was caught by pole-and-line fishing in 1993. It had a smooth, unforgettable deliciousness with a subtle aroma and soft sweetness that's different from large *shibi*.

The *oma*'s popularity is increasing drastically lately. Before the great earthquake that hit southwest offshore Hokkaido, *shibi* from Teuri Island (in the Sea of Japan) had a good reputation, but we can no longer seem to catch any, maybe because the course for the fish at the bottom of the sea has changed. Now if it's called "*oma*," then regardless of its size, the bid price hikes up.

That's because the fishermen in Oma use poles and lines to catch *maguro* that have feasted on squid off the coast of Hokkaido and gained plenty of fat and are now prowling the strait for more food. After landing one, the gents immediately haul it to port, so they get paid well. This is why the freshness, fattiness, and coloring is good, but that forty-kilo *chubo* was the best by far.

There is a clear difference in taste between *ipponzuri* (pole-and-line fishing) and the predominant *haenawa* (longline) method of catching *maguro*. I compared them with my palate and came to this conclusion.

That's to say, those *maguro* swimming in shallow waters that aren't too

big are the ones caught by *ipponzuri* (pole-and-line fishing), *hikinawa* (seine fishing), *makiami* (round-haul netting), and *teichiami* (fixed-net fishing). I prefer smallish *maguro* that weigh under 150 kilos that are landed by pole-and-line fishing. It's not too fatty and has a nice aroma and tastes smooth. It will be impeccable if it's from Hokkaido or Aomori in season. The fishermen around that area know what to do with their catch.

On the other hand, *haenawa* (longline fishing) sets hooks to target big ocean *maguro*. This is why it tends to have too much fat and tastes greasy.

I have other reasons why I don't like *'nawa*.

Maguro doesn't breathe by opening and closing its gills. Like *katsuo* (bonito), it swims with its mouth half open and forces seawater into its gills to take in oxygen. It can't survive unless it keeps swimming.

So when it gets caught by a hook, it dies after struggling and suffering. I will omit a detailed explanation, but when this happens, its body temperature rises drastically and apparently burns its own flesh.

With *haenawa*, they set a long line over a 100-to-150-kilometer-wide area of the sea, so from the time they set the first hook to the last hook, we're talking about over twenty hours. There is no way *maguro* caught on an early hook can remain in good condition.

When I cut out a *saku* (slab), the coloring of the lean meat looks better than expected. It looks good, but when I try it, it's slick and tastes too plain, as expected. The only fat is oddly greasy. There is no umami whatsoever to the point that I begin to wonder why.

When they haul in the *'nawa*, if the last hooks yielded a catch then it's been only four to five hours, and the freshness is fine then, but that's a pretty low percentage. In any case, I think there are many bad-quality *maguro* caught by *'nawa*.

However, it's true that in this day and age we don't have the luxury to prefer "fishing" over "longlines." They can't catch any in the seas near Japan, so it's eye-poppingly expensive.

Everyone says, "There is no question that it tastes good, but it's way too expensive." I agree, but because of demand and supply, the price continues to rise.

We can't charge that much for a mere nigiri

The highest price reached in Tsukiji Market was the first bid of the year in 1996: 9,040,000 yen for one *maguro*. It was for a 238-kilo one from off the coast of Kishu. Back then, for two weeks including the New Year's off days, we couldn't get ahold of *kinkai hon maguro* at all, so I was half ready to concede on January 5th, the first day of work—"I have no choice but to go for frozen."

On a day like that, one *shibi* came into the market, so there was a big commotion. Two brokers who specialize in premium *maguro* held their ground and kept hiking up the bids.

Their top customers aren't high-end traditional restaurants, but a small number of sushi restaurants that can't open without *kinkai hon maguro*. They don't deal just with Sukiyabashi Jiro. There are a few chefs. This is why the brokers come on strong.

In any case, sushi restaurants with whom they have long relationships desperately want it, so neither side is willing to lose. And this is why in no time, the price exceeds 9,000,000 yen.

However, even the *maguro* broker who wins isn't happy with the high price.

Leading brokers have several stores, so no matter how big the *shibi* is, they can easily sell it. It's easy, but to put aside the math, the minimum unit for sushi restaurants will be 500,000 yen. No matter which block you buy, from *harakami*, which includes *otoro*, to the tail part that's sinewy, it costs 500,000 yen.

The broker divides the fish, the buyers draw lots, and they're paired up, but no matter how desperate, no sushi chef buys such astronomically expensive *shibi*, especially the sinewy tail part, with a smile on his face.

So the broker who emerges victorious will have to sell at a discount. He's ready to forgo profit as he bids up the price. "I don't want to lose to my rival." "I want to make my sushi restaurant clients happy." It's sheer professional pride. He's disregarding profit and loss from the outset.

It's not just brokers—all those concerned are crying. To have caught only one in two weeks means most of the tens and hundreds of *maguro* fishing boats that set sail on the winter ocean came back empty-handed. The captains of the boats buy expensive fuel and live bait, then pay their fishermen, and then they only caught one fish.

To begin with, that *maguro* wasn't worth the "new record" price at all. There was no *shibi* during those two weeks. It was extremely scarce. That was the only reason the cost shot up to 9,040,000 yen.

Because if it's that big, then the sinew in the belly is too strong to chew off. And that sinew takes up a third of the *otoro* portion. Once all the sinew is removed, the *neta*'s price climbs to 5,000 yen to 6,000 yen per piece. Peel the skin off. Debone it. Remove the red muscle. If the lean meat is too sleek and can't be used, then things get even bleaker. If we were to charge the market price, it'd be 10,000 yen per nigiri. For a pair, 20,000 yen.

We can't charge that kind of price for mere nigiri. Hence, no matter how high the cost, I only charge 2,500 yen, as usual. I'm ready for a big loss. The master of a sushi restaurant has his pride, too.

"Do you have *otoro*?"

"Well, I couldn't afford it because it was stupidly expensive. I'm sorry, but we are out of it today."

There is no way I can say this as someone who hawks his *kinkai hon maguro*.

"I see, I see. But such-and-such was making nigiri with it. Hahahaha."

At 7 a.m., after stocking the restaurant, he attaches an 80-kg load onto the carrier and heads back. He has continued this every day for over thirty years.

If I were mockingly laughed at like that, where would it leave me?

At that time, what we won from drawing lots was the middle of the back portion. The part called "*se no naka*" doesn't include *otoro*. So I wonder how much we lost. A huge amount, I'm sure.

But we already knew that. "Even if we sold all of it, it'd add up to only this much in revenue." A ballpark estimate. Times like that, you can't do detailed accounting. It just feels stupid. I am, after all, a business manager, and it's not that I don't think about profit. But there is nothing you can do when scarce *shibi* fetches a crazy price. I decided not to do the math.

If you estimate the ratios of *otoro*, *chutoro*, and lean meat for a *saku* (slab), tally how many *saku* each comes out to, and consider that the selling price of lean meat is a fifth of *otoro*…you can calculate the cost that way. You can, but if that's what's on your mind, the slices keep getting thinner and the *shari* keeps getting bigger, and you can't make delicious nigiri.

I don't like to talk about prices. Once we who're making the nigiri start to worry about that, we end up getting all stingy.

Let's say one *maguro saku* normally costs 10,000 yen. But then you learn, "It costs 40,000 yen today."

"Okay, it costs four times more. Let me make the *neta* thinner and make two or three pieces extra."

It could get that way. Of course, there's a huge difference between 10,000 yen and 40,000 yen. If you sliced four extra pieces out of a *saku* and sold them for 2,000 yen apiece, you'd make an extra 8,000 yen. Then, even if the cost is four times higher, the margin of error shrinks.

If you keep calculating that way, then of course the *maguro* slices get thinner.

When I make nigiri with *toro*, I prioritize the balance between *neta* and *shari* and adjust the thickness of the slice. This is because I'm considering how to make the best-tasting nigiri. If I make nigiri with *otoro* of the same thickness as *chutoro*, then it might be too rich. I might slice it thinner for that reason.

That's why when a customer sticks around forever and blithely orders only the *maguro*, *shinko* (young gizzard shad), *kuruma ebi* (prawn), and *uni* (sea urchin) that I'm serving at my "bleeding price," to be honest, I'm fuming at heart. Even now that I'm over seventy.

"Bastard! You have no idea how I feel."

I'm no spring chicken, but I still run a business.

But don't be surprised by 9,040,000 yen. There is always something that's more expensive.

That *shibi* from off Kishu cost 39,140 yen per kilo. That's surely expensive, but it's actually not startling.

The highest price per kilo at Tsukiji was 46,350 yen on November 20, 1996. After removing the skin, bones, and red muscle tissue and simply calculating the yield rate at sixty percent, you reach the unreasonable cost-price of 7,725 yen per 100 grams, but I'm sure this record will be renewed continuously.

I'll study extra hard about imported *maguro* from now on

There is one more troubling issue. Some people say, "*Maguro* from the seas near Japan is delicious" and "The imported ones taste bad." This "*kinkai hon maguro* supremacy" is rampant.

"Why do they praise *kinkai* (nearby seas) so much, and in contrast, regard imported ones, especially frozen *maguro*, as inferior?"

Even I, who insist on *kinkai hon maguro*, feel that this deep-rooted trend, prevalent among customers and also sushi craftsmen, is something we could almost call a creed. This belief that "If it's not *kinkai*, then it's not *hon maguro* (blue fin tuna) at all" came about gradually, maybe led on by sushi restaurants or the *maguro* brokers. It's really a strange story.

What I mean is, when we say "imported," for instance, the ones that land in Los Angeles are the exact same authentic *hon maguro* that were swimming in the seas near Japan. It's just that it swam across the Pacific Ocean from Japan to Los Angeles and got caught there.

As soon as the same *maguro* is labeled as being "from off the coast of Los Angeles," people say, "Heck, it's imported," so it's troubling. This is what I tell them: In the summertime, when the ones around Japan are skinny after the spawning season, the ones over there are fat and taste good.

Even people who understand this in their heads might be thinking, "LA? No way," deep down. As sushi chefs, then, we have no choice but to desperately search for *kinkai*.

This is why the fate of *kinkai hon maguro* as a natural resource is a severe and dire issue for the master of a sushi restaurant.

In the past, when the brokers had low stock, they offered *kinkai hon maguro* that had been frozen in season. However, lately they sell out while they are fresh, leaving none for the warehouse. So almost all the frozen *maguro* are from overseas.

Even if they've been frozen, Pacific *maguro* and *minami maguro* (southern bluefin tuna) are far superior to the domestic *mebachi* (bigeye tuna) or *kihada* (yellowfin tuna).

People have said for a long time, "*Nyubai mebachi* (bigeye tuna in mid-June) is in season so it's delicious." But I don't agree with that. I actually ate them to compare them. *Mebachi* doesn't have strong fat at all, even in the bellows belly of *otoro*—it has grease, but not richness of flavor. It's like drinking bland hot water instead of tea. Only a dry and unsatisfied feel remains in the mouth. Just like with boiled barley rice.

Kihada is a fish that's popular in Kansai. But as a nigiri *neta*, it's like "reheated porridge" and not on the same level as *hon maguro*, which is like

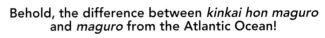

Behold, the difference between *kinkai hon maguro* and *maguro* from the Atlantic Ocean!

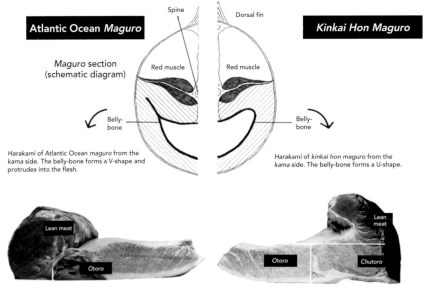

Spine

Dorsal fin

Atlantic Ocean *Maguro*

Kinkai Hon Maguro

Maguro section
(schematic diagram)

Red muscle

Red muscle

Belly-bone

Belly-bone

Harakami of Atlantic Ocean *maguro* from the kama side. The belly-bone forms a V-shape and protrudes into the flesh.

Harakami of *kinkai hon maguro* from the kama side. The belly-bone forms a U-shape.

Lean meat

Lean meat

Otoro

Otoro

Chutoro

Both *kinkai hon maguro* and Atlantic Ocean *maguro* (commonly known as jumbo *maguro*) are "bluefin tunas" and look the same to the common eye. However, when you examine their sections, you can clearly see the difference. The schematic diagram above shows the section behind the gills, and when you compare them, the belly-bone of Atlantic Ocean *maguro* forms a V-shape and protrudes at a sharp angle deep into the flesh. In other words, the belly-bone of Atlantic Ocean *maguro* divides the *toro* and lean meat, and you can't obtain any *chutoro*, with its contrast of fat. You can see this from the cross sections of *harakami*. *Chutoro* is a part unique to *kinkai hon maguro*. The belly-bones of Mediterranean *maguro* and Indian *maguro* protrude in the same way as the Atlantic Ocean variety's.

"freshly cooked rice." Whether it's fresh or frozen, from the Pacific Ocean or the Atlantic Ocean, or even the Mediterranean, no matter where it was landed, *hon maguro* is still "the King of Sushi."

For instance, in the winter when good-quality *kinkai shibi* is scarce, if I make nigiri with defrosted imported *maguro,* well, I wonder how many people have the discerning palate to call it and say, "This isn't *kinkai hon maguro.*"

Even if it's frozen, fatty in-season *maguro* tastes far better than *kinkai shibi* that's out of season and skinny. It doesn't even have to be the ones from

Los Angeles that swam from Japan or the jumbo raw ones that fly in from New York.

Even though they are both *hon maguro*, *kinkai hon maguro* and foreign *maguro* are different types. In particular, the Atlantic *hon maguro* is different in its bone structure.

The *kinkai* has a sleek, elongated trunk. The ones from the Atlantic Ocean are pudgy. And whether it's from Oma or Los Angeles, once its head is cut off, you see a continuous *harakami* (upper belly portion) that includes *chutoro* and *shimofuri* (marbled flesh)—but not so with the Atlantic variety. The belly-bone in the *harakami* sticks out into the lean meat, so the *chutoro* that exists in *kinkai hon maguro* isn't there. All of a sudden, it's *otoro*.

Of course, they have different flavors. It's almost as different as vegetable oil and lard. You can tell if you actually eat and compare them. The fat is strong in *kinkai hon maguro*, but it tastes smooth. It's not greasy, and it has a nice aftertaste.

However, the fat of *hon maguro* from the Atlantic Ocean and *minami maguro* (southern bluefin tuna) tastes very rich, like lard. It lacks the refreshing, mouth-cleansing aroma. The flesh is hard. The sinew is tough.

It depends on the *maguro*'s size, but if you let *kinkai* rest for a while, the sinew disappears. But with the other ones, no matter how long you let it rest, the sinew remains.

So if it's too greasy, slice it thinner. If it's too tough, remove the sinew. If not, carve out the flesh between the sinews. That's how you could make nigiri with it, even though there's more waste for sure that way.

Customers who are used to eating *kinkai hon maguro* that's like "vegetable oil" might think, "What? This is a bit too greasy" in the beginning. But once they get used to it, they won't mind the richness of "lard." You can take away the discomfort by going the extra mile with your craft.

I think so.

After all, *shibi* is "the King of Sushi." Without its appetite-stimulating color, our *neta* box will look dumb.

"When *kinkai hon maguro* is gone for good, *Jiro* will close," some regulars worry in earnest. But these days, this is how I answer them: "Nope—like I'd take down my *Sukiyabashi Jiro* sign so soon."

How to turn "lard" into smooth "vegetable oil."
I'll have you know that I've started studying extra hard about imported *maguro*.

Chapter 3

Prepping the Four Seasons' Nigiri

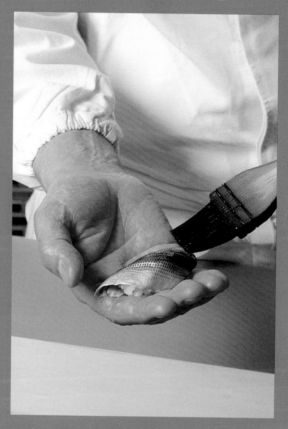

We asked Jiro Ono, "Please let us photograph your preparation process in every detail." For a sushi restaurant, the flavoring of *tane* is a corporate secret akin to arcane lore handed down through a family. We were ready for him to refuse. However, to our surprise, he simply answered, "Oh, sure. Come whenever you'd like."

Take this as a rare opportunity to relish a master's mysterious rituals, be it for *tako* (octopus), *shako* (mantis shrimp), *awabi* (abalone), *tamagoyaki* (Japanese omelette), or *nitsume* (reduction sauce) and *nikiri* (thin and sweet glaze).

Silver-Skinned Fish

One nigiri at a time, served on a black lacquered plate.

Kohada (gizzard shad), *maruzuke*, May, Kyushu

One whole fish per nigiri, i.e. *maruzuke*-size, throughout the year.

❶ Right before making nigiri, place *kohada* (gizzard shad) slanted on the palm.

❷ Twist tail to express liveliness.

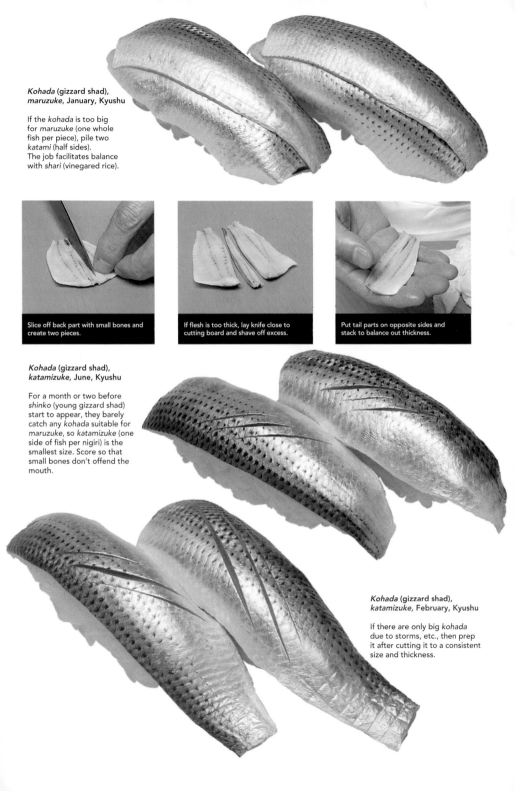

Kohada (gizzard shad),
maruzuke, January, Kyushu

If the *kohada* is too big
for *maruzuke* (one whole
fish per piece), pile two
katami (half sides).
The job facilitates balance
with *shari* (vinegared rice).

Slice off back part with small bones and create two pieces.

If flesh is too thick, lay knife close to cutting board and shave off excess.

Put tail parts on opposite sides and stack to balance out thickness.

Kohada (gizzard shad),
katamizuke, June, Kyushu

For a month or two before
shinko (young gizzard shad)
start to appear, they barely
catch any *kohada* suitable for
maruzuke, so *katamizuke* (one
side of fish per nigiri) is the
smallest size. Score so that
small bones don't offend the
mouth.

Kohada (gizzard shad),
katamizuke, February, Kyushu

If there are only big *kohada*
due to storms, etc., then prep
it after cutting it to a consistent
size and thickness.

Shinko (young gizzard shad),
two per nigiri,
mid-August, Ariake Sea

The small ones called *shinko*
are available until around this
time. Compared to the size,
the flesh is still so thin that
you can see the rice grains.

Shinko (young gizzard shad),
one and a half per nigiri,
late August, Ariake Sea

Though big enough to make
nigiri as *maruzuke*, the flesh
is too thin. Add one *katami*.

Silver-Skinned Fish

konoshiro

Shinko (young gizzard shad),
maruzuke, September,
Ariake Sea

Around this season, it's called
shinko but tastes like *kohada*.
But compared to May *kohada*
(page 160), it tastes lighter.

Shinko (young gizzard shad), four per nigiri,
early August, Ariake Sea (Saga Prefecture)

A nigiri using four pieces of young *kohada* 5 to 6 cm long.
After prepping, each fish is only as long as the width of the
sushi topping.

To make thickness even, pile one upon
another like armor.

Shinko (young gizzard
shad), three per nigiri,
early August,
Ariake Sea

Shinko this size is good
to eat at 6 to 7 p.m. after
prepping in the morning.

nakazumi

kohada (maruzuke-size,
one per nigiri)

shinko (two per nigiri)

shinko (four per nigiri)

Aji (horse mackerel) (raw), July,
Tokyo Bay (Chiba Prefecture)

Two pieces of nigiri per *katami* (one side).
Because it's fatty, the distinctive red color
of the flesh is paler. Score the tail to make
it look nicer. For *aji*, insert *shoga* (ginger),
not wasabi.

Aji (horse mackerel) (raw),
July, Tokyo Bay
(Chiba Prefecture)

For silver-skin-averse guests,
slice off flesh on head side
so it doesn't stand out.

Aji (horse mackerel)
(raw, one side per nigiri), May,
Tokyo Bay (Chiba Prefecture)

Koaji make one piece for each side.
The silver skin looks bad around
now, so score flesh to make it look
better.

Aji (horse mackerel)
(pickled, one side, marinated)

Recreated work from the old days.
Salt and pickle, and without peeling
skin, insert *oboro* (ground cooked
flesh) to make nigiri. Removing
thorn-like scale without damaging
skin surface requires skill.

164

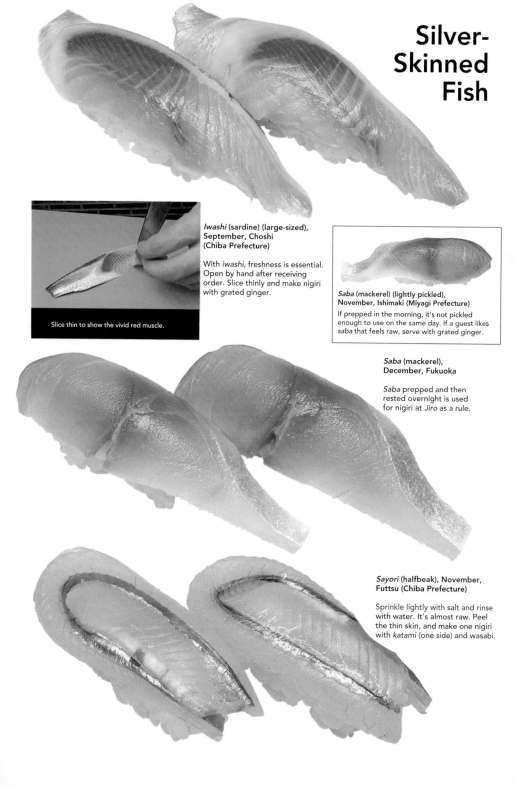

Silver-Skinned Fish

**Iwashi (sardine) (large-sized),
September, Choshi
(Chiba Prefecture)**

With *iwashi*, freshness is essential.
Open by hand after receiving
order. Slice thinly and make nigiri
with grated ginger.

Slice thin to show the vivid red muscle.

Saba (mackerel) (lightly pickled),
November, Ishimaki (Miyagi Prefecture)

If prepped in the morning, it's not pickled
enough to use on the same day. If a guest likes
saba that feels raw, serve with grated ginger.

**Saba (mackerel),
December, Fukuoka**

Saba prepped and then
rested overnight is used
for nigiri at *Jiro* as a rule.

**Sayori (halfbeak), November,
Futtsu (Chiba Prefecture)**

Sprinkle lightly with salt and rinse
with water. It's almost raw. Peel
the thin skin, and make one nigiri
with *katami* (one side) and wasabi.

Whitefish

Suzuki (sea bass), August, Joban

The name changes as the fish gets bigger: *seigo* to *fukko* to *suzuki*. It has a singular flavor within a plain taste. This is one size bigger than early spring *fukko* and fatty.

55 cm long, slightly under 1.5 kg. A smallish *suzuki*.

A lot of the belly-bone part is cut out because it can smell like petroleum.

Mako Garei (marbled sole), May, Joban

By the time the flesh of *hirame* (flounder) turns dull and white, *mako garei* start to fatten. The staple whitefish during spring and summer.

Fukko (young sea bass), June, Joban

Weighs 1.2 kg per fish. Starts in early spring. Compared to *mako garei*'s (marbled sole) firmer flesh, it's soft.

Mako Garei (marbled sole), top, and *Hirame* (flounder)

Soge (young flounder), September, Aomori

Hirame offspring weighing under a kilo are called *soge*. Fills the gap until 2-kg-range *hirame* start to fatten. It has a plainer flavor.

**Hirame (flounder),
February, Aomori**

The King of Whitefish from autumn to
winter. The 2-kg *hirame* is best for the
flesh's richness and thickness.
When fatty, the flesh turns amber-colored.

"Out of all the toppings, *hirame* is the most
satisfying to make nigiri with," says Jiro.

Engawa (little flesh on the fin) of *Hirame,* March, Aomori

A rare item: only enough to make fourteen nigiri per 2-kg *hirame*.
It's at the root of the fin and moves a lot, so the muscle is developed.
Resilient, chewy texture.

Slicing *engawa* into nigiri-*dane*.

Colored
Fish

* Some places
categorize it
as whitefish,
but considered
"colored" at *Jiro*.

*Tennen Shima Aji
wild striped jack), September,
Katsuyama (Chiba Prefecture)*

t used to be considered even more
remium than *tai* (sea bream) before
armed ones started to come to market.
Often categorized as whitefish, it's
olored fish with a coloring in between
white and red meat.

Wild *shima aji* from Tokyo
Bay that weighs 700 grams

Inada
(young yellowtail),
February, Tateyama
(Chiba Prefecture)

In the season of *kan buri*
(cold season yellowtail), *inada*
(young *buri*) also gets fatty.

Colored
Fish

Inada
From Misaki on Miura
Peninsula. 1.5 kg

Inada (young yellowtail),
April, Misaki (Kanagawa
Prefecture)

Unlike farmed *hamachi* (yellowtail),
there is redness to the wild flesh.
It also has a tight texture.

Wakashi, May, Misaki

Buri is a fish that changes
its name from *wakashi* to
inada to *warasa* to *buri*.
This is from the back of a
wakashi weighing about 1.1 kg.
The coloring is even redder
than *inada*.

Shokko (young greater amberjack),
October, Tokyo Bay

Young *kanpachi* (greater amberjack)
is called *shokko*. *Kanpachi* has
a texture similar to *buri*
but has its own aroma.

Wild *shokko*
(young greater amberjack)
from Tokyo Bay, 700 g

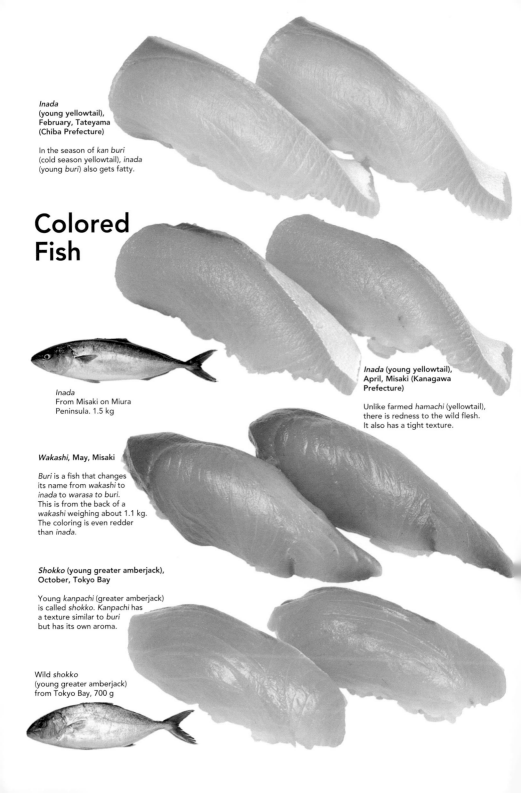

Lean Meat

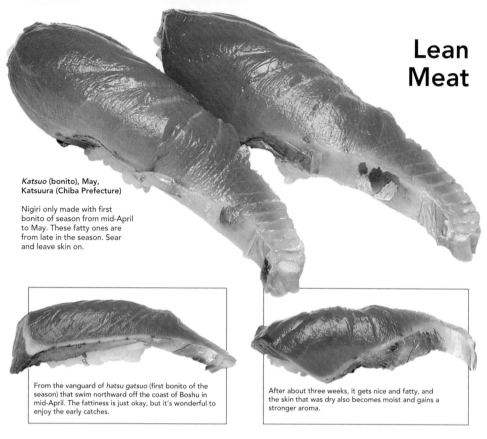

Katsuo (bonito), May,
Katsuura (Chiba Prefecture)

Nigiri only made with first
bonito of season from mid-April
to May. These fatty ones are
from late in the season. Sear
and leave skin on.

From the vanguard of *hatsu gatsuo* (first bonito of the
season) that swim northward off the coast of Boshu in
mid-April. The fattiness is just okay, but it's wonderful to
enjoy the early catches.

After about three weeks, it gets nice and fatty, and
the skin that was dry also becomes moist and gains a
stronger aroma.

Grill skin over a straw fire. The heat is low so it doesn't go
through to the flesh.

After skin is grilled, add more straw and smoke
the flesh side with cloud of smoke.

Insert chopped chives and grated ginger and
make nigiri.

Squid

Sumi Ika (squid), March, Nagasaki

Use ones that make from four pieces up to about seven or eight at the largest for the month of March. When April arrives, they start to have offspring and get skinny.

Koika (small squid), early August, Izumi (Kagoshima Prefecture)

Sumi ika offspring with flesh so thin you can see through to the wasabi, and so soft that it melts in the mouth.

The width of *koika* (small squid) and the length of nigiri become exactly the same. Make nigiri with it as if to wrap the vinegared rice.

Peel thin skin off front and back and slice vertically into two parts.

Koika from Izumi in Kagoshima Prefecture. Torso measures only 7 cm.

Koika (small squid), *warizuke* (one for two pieces), mid August, Izumi

Koika for two pieces of nigiri has sufficient thickness, nice texture, and the umami of *sumi ika*.

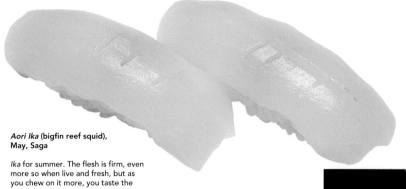

Aori Ika (bigfin reef squid),
May, Saga

Ika for summer. The flesh is firm, even
more so when live and fresh, but as
you chew on it more, you taste the
sweetness.

Geso (squid tentacles) of *Koika* (small squid), August, Izumi

For guests who eschew sweet *nitsume* (reduction sauce),
serve it with *nikiri* (thin and sweet glaze) and wasabi.

The flesh is thick, so slice it thin and pound
on it with base of knife.

Geso (tentacles) of *Koika* (small squid),
August, Izumi

Warizuke (one for two pieces)-size
koika tentacles. After boiling, peel skin
and cut off tip. Make nigiri without
wasabi and with nitsume brushed on it.

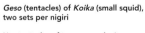

Geso (tentacles) of *Koika* (small squid),
two sets per nigiri

Use tentacles of two *maruzuke* (one
per piece)-size *koika* to make nigiri.
With the tentacles of koika, which are
small, you don't so much as boil as run
them through boiling water.

171

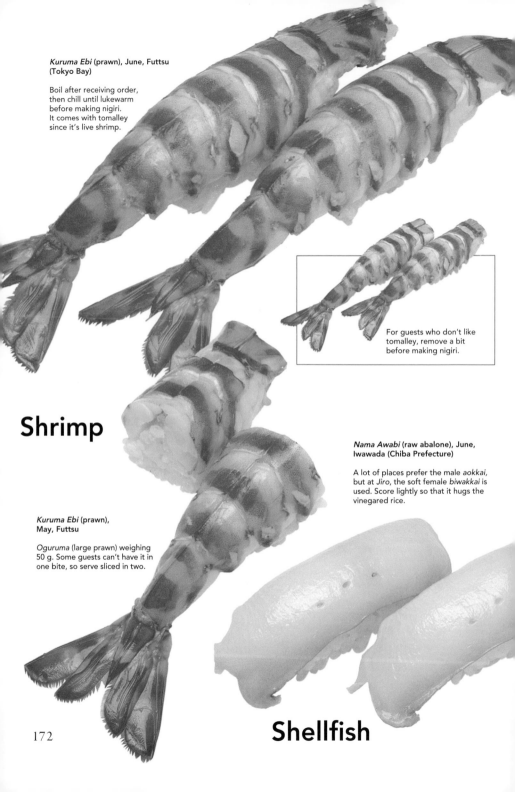

Kuruma Ebi (prawn), June, Futtsu
(Tokyo Bay)

Boil after receiving order,
then chill until lukewarm
before making nigiri.
It comes with tomalley
since it's live shrimp.

For guests who don't like
tomalley, remove a bit
before making nigiri.

Shrimp

Kuruma Ebi (prawn),
May, Futtsu

Oguruma (large prawn) weighing
50 g. Some guests can't have it in
one bite, so serve sliced in two.

Nama Awabi (raw abalone), June,
Iwawada (Chiba Prefecture)

A lot of places prefer the male *aokkai*,
but at *Jiro*, the soft female *biwakkai* is
used. Score lightly so that it hugs the
vinegared rice.

Shellfish

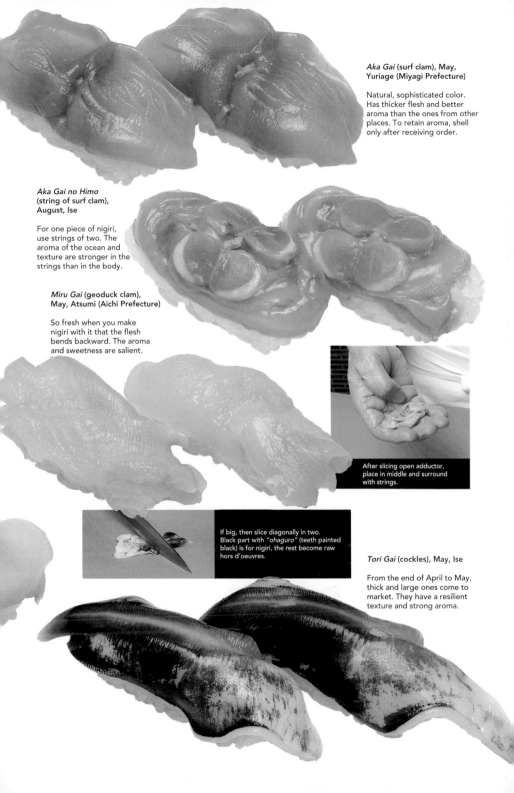

Aka Gai (surf clam), May, Yuriage (Miyagi Prefecture)

Natural, sophisticated color. Has thicker flesh and better aroma than the ones from other places. To retain aroma, shell only after receiving order.

Aka Gai no Himo (string of surf clam), August, Ise

For one piece of nigiri, use strings of two. The aroma of the ocean and texture are stronger in the strings than in the body.

Miru Gai (geoduck clam), May, Atsumi (Aichi Prefecture)

So fresh when you make nigiri with it that the flesh bends backward. The aroma and sweetness are salient.

After slicing open adductor, place in middle and surround with strings.

If big, then slice diagonally in two. Black part with *"ohaguro"* (teeth painted black) is for nigiri, the rest become raw hors d'oeuvres.

Tori Gai (cockles), May, Ise

From the end of April to May, thick and large ones come to market. They have a resilient texture and strong aroma.

Simmered Items

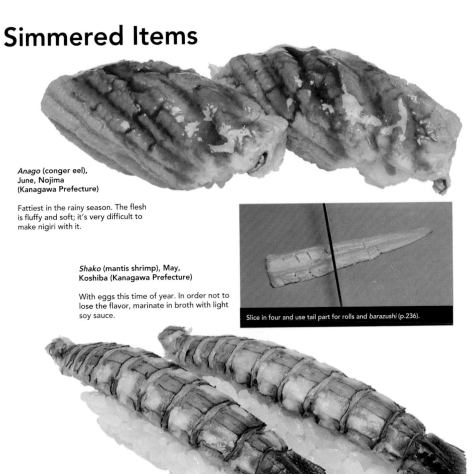

Anago (conger eel),
June, Nojima
(Kanagawa Prefecture)

Fattiest in the rainy season. The flesh
is fluffy and soft; it's very difficult to
make nigiri with it.

Shako (mantis shrimp), May,
Koshiba (Kanagawa Prefecture)

With eggs this time of year. In order not to
lose the flavor, marinate in broth with light
soy sauce.

Slice in four and use tail part for rolls and *barazushi* (p.236).

A cross-section of *shako*: the orange part are
eggs, and with this many, there's barely any
flesh.

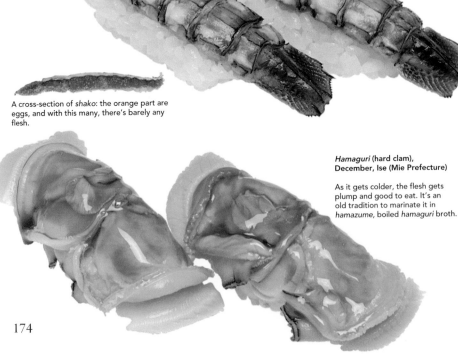

Hamaguri (hard clam),
December, Ise (Mie Prefecture)

As it gets colder, the flesh gets
plump and good to eat. It's an
old tradition to marinate it in
hamazume, boiled *hamaguri* broth.

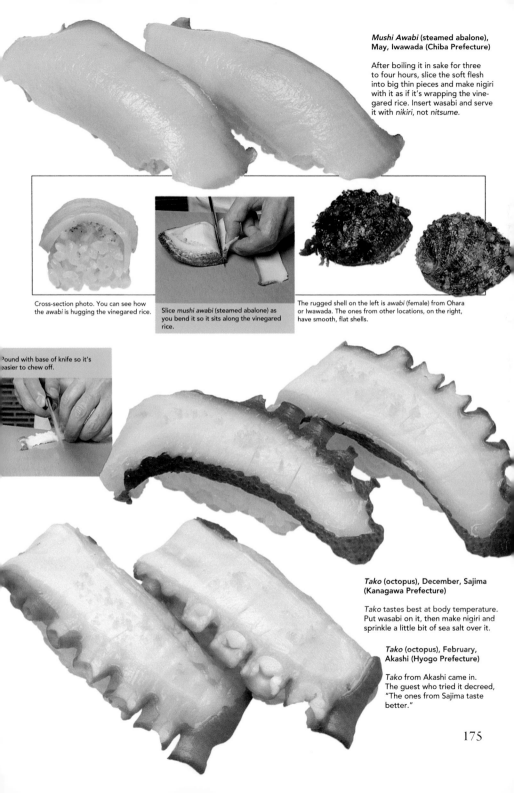

Mushi Awabi (steamed abalone), May, Iwawada (Chiba Prefecture)

After boiling it in sake for three to four hours, slice the soft flesh into big thin pieces and make nigiri with it as if it's wrapping the vinegared rice. Insert wasabi and serve it with *nikiri*, not *nitsume*.

Cross-section photo. You can see how the *awabi* is hugging the vinegared rice.

Slice *mushi awabi* (steamed abalone) as you bend it so it sits along the vinegared rice.

The rugged shell on the left is *awabi* (female) from Ohara or Iwawada. The ones from other locations, on the right, have smooth, flat shells.

Pound with base of knife so it's easier to chew off.

Tako (octopus), December, Sajima (Kanagawa Prefecture)

Tako tastes best at body temperature. Put wasabi on it, then make nigiri and sprinkle a little bit of sea salt over it.

Tako (octopus), February, Akashi (Hyogo Prefecture)

Tako from Akashi came in. The guest who tried it decreed, "The ones from Sajima taste better."

175

Uni (sea urchin),
June, Hokkaido

At *Jiro*, it's mainly
ezo murasaki uni.
It has a less creamy
texture but tastes
light.

Gunkan Maki

(nigiri wrapped in *nori*
with the *neta* on top)

Uni from Kudamatsu (Tokuyama Bay). Strong aroma of the ocean
and a unique smooth flavor. Unfortunate drawback: wooden box's
smell often transfers to *uni*.

The edible part of *uni* are its ovaries, and
you get five clumps out of one shell.

Ikura (salmon roe),
October, Sanriku

Soy sauce-marinated raw
ikura doesn't have the
fishy smell of *shio ikura*
(salted salmon row). Prep
for the whole year in-season to enjoy the umami
throughout the year.

Kobashira (small scallops),
May, Hokkaido

The pale, large pieces called
oboshi (large star), rather than
the small, darker ones from
Futtsu. The latter have a nice
flavor and aroma but fell out of
favor because they contain sand.

Work of Sukiyabashi Jiro

Follow His Preparation Process

Shima Aji
(striped jack)

(fillet into three)

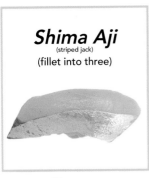

Wild *shima aji* from Katsuyama in Chiba Prefecture, 700 g

A farmed *shima aji* for comparison. Fatter than the wild one.

With *debabocho* (broad-bladed kitchen knife), scrape off *zengo* (thorn-like scale) trying not to damage surface of silver skin. ❶

Remove scales, scraping in reverse direction with tip of knife. ❷

Cut off head behind pectoral fin. ❸

Cut belly open up to anal fin and remove innards. ❹

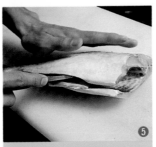

Rinse belly with water, and then insert knife above spine and cut open to root of tail. ❺

Do the same for back side; slide knife above spine and slice half of flesh off of spine. ❻

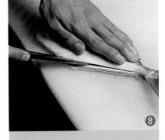

Place *shima aji* spine side down and insert knife along spine from back. ❼

Then from belly, cut open along spine. ❽

Hold knife with blade facing away and slice flesh off of spine to root of tail. ❾

At root of tail, cut off flesh. ❿

Two slices of flesh and one with bones: filleted into three.

Switch to *yanagiba* (kitchen knife for sashimi) and carve out belly-bone while lightly pressing down with left fingers.

Remove bones and bones only, and none of the flesh.

Insert knife along impression of spine and separate belly portion.

Chop off edge of tail side and start to peel skin from there. Insert knife in between skin and flesh and peel skin.

The flesh from the back and belly is called *jomi*.

Cut off red muscle and get back portion.

The *jomi* of farmed *shima aji*: less translucent.

179

Mako Garei
(marbled sole)

(fillet into five)

Raise pectoral fin, insert *debabocho* (broad-bladed kitchen knife), and cut off head.

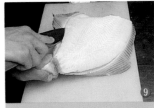

Likewise, with blading facing away, slice opposite side from tail toward head.

Mako garei from Joban, 1.5 kg

Remove innards and insert knife along rib bones.

Insert knife to spine and slice along lateral line of fish.

Comb out scales with *yanagiba* (kitchen knife for sashimi).

Scrape out red muscles located at backbone with tip of *debabocho*.

Lifting up flesh from fin's base, slice along rib bones with knife. Cut off and completely separate first fillet.

Slide knife carefully so as not to damage the flesh.

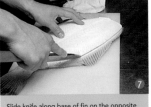

Slide knife along base of fin on the opposite side.

Do the same for white-skinned belly side.

Lift up tail, hold knife with blade facing away, and slice along rib bones.

Insert knife along other side of spine.

180

Lifting up flesh, slice along rib bones with knife and cut off second fillet.

Comb out belly-bone carefully.

With the bones facing down, make cut along base of both fins.

Likewise, slice off fourth fillet.

Chop off parts with strong sinews.

Cut down to spine.

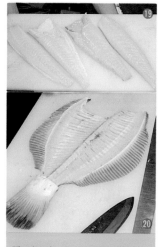

Filleted into five pieces total, four of flesh and one with bones.

Peel a little bit of skin at tail. Pulling skin hard, insert knife between flesh and skin and peel as if pressing skin onto cutting board.

Chop off tail at base.

Lifting up flesh, slice off third fillet.

For each flesh piece, slice off *engawa* (root of fin) with *yanagiba*.

181

Kohada
(gizzard shad)

Kohada, from Kyushu, *maruzuke*-size

With *debabocho* (broad-bladed kitchen knife),
raise fin and cut off at root. **❶**

Scrape off scales with tip of knife. **❷**

With the pectoral fin and behind the black dot
as your guide, chop off head. **❸**

Chop off edge of belly right up to anal fin. **❹**

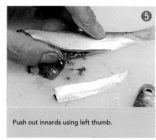

❺ Push out innards using left thumb.

❻ Chop off tail at root.

❼ Insert knife above spine and slice toward
tail in one go.

❽ Insert knife between spine and flesh and slice
off and separate flesh from spine.

Slice
off
belly-
bone. **❾**

❿ Sort by size, thickness, and fattiness.

Sprinkle
salt on
bonzaru
(wicker
colander). **⓫**

⓬ Beginning with large *kohada*, arrange onto
bonzaru skin-side down.

Sprinkle salt
until *kohada* is
slightly white.

⓭

182

After five minutes, sprinkle salt on another *bonzaru* and arrange small *kohada*.

Place on *zaru* (wicker colander) and drain. Try not to mix small and large.

Put each size into separate *zaru* and drain vinegar.

Sprinkle them with salt, using less salt than for large *kohada*.

Stand them against colander, cover with plastic wrap, and let rest overnight in refrigerator.

Let them rest for twenty-five minutes for large ones, twenty minutes for small ones.

Rinse with vinegar once to wash away fishiness and sliminess, and put back on colander.

Soak large *kohada* in vinegar, and five minutes later put small *kohada* in another bowl of vinegar.

Rinse both large and small ones and wash away the salt.

Flesh starts to turn white after twenty minutes.

Top: right after pickling and still raw
Bottom: good to eat after a day

183

Shinko
(young gizzard shad)

Sort into three by size, thickness, and fat content.

Soak pieces in salt water: big ones for four and a half minutes, medium for three minutes, small ones for two and a half minutes.

Soak shinko in salt water with ice cubes.

Rinse with salt water with ice cubes to prevent flesh from becoming watery.

Make three bowls of strongly salted water with ice cubes.

Put the shinko in colander and drain.

Cut dorsal fin and remove scales.

Slice along spine with knife and open flesh.

Rinse with vinegar by size.

Chop off head and belly and remove innards.

Insert knife between spine and flesh and slice off and separate flesh from spine.

Slice off belly-bone. Be careful not to take off too much since the flesh is thin.

Soak in vinegar: big ones for four and a half minutes, medium for three minutes, small ones for two minutes.

Drain vinegar and arrange shinko in colander, large ones first. Prepped in the morning, it's good to eat by evening.

Aji
(horse mackerel)

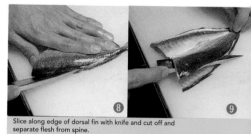

Slice along edge of dorsal fin with knife and cut off and separate flesh from spine.

Maaji, fished *aji* from Futtsu, 120 g

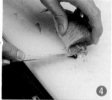

Remove innards. With fresh ones, just pulling does it.

Cut off spine at root of tail. Do not chop off tail yet.

With *debabocho* (broad-bladed kitchen knife), slice off *zengo* (thorn like scale).

Scrape away any that's left and rinse fish with water.

Press down anal fin with knife, pull flesh, and extract entire bone.

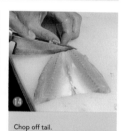

Chop off tail.

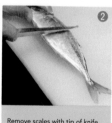

Remove scales with tip of knife.

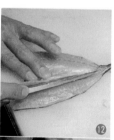

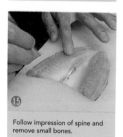

Follow impression of spine and remove small bones.

Cut off head diagonally from behind pectoral fin.

Insert knife by dorsal fin, slide knife along spine, and open flesh.

Slice off belly-bone.

Saba
(mackerel)

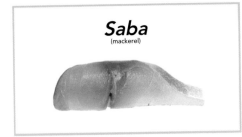

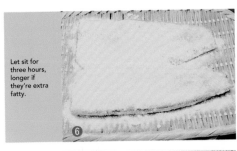

Let sit for three hours, longer if they're extra fatty.

⑥

Masaba from Fukuoka, 800 g

⑦

Place *saba* in water and wash away salt.

⑧

Drain, placing *saba* on the colander.

❶

Fillet *saba* into three.

❸

Place a *bonzaru* (wicker colander) on top of a bowl and arrange flesh of *saba*.

⑨

Soak in vinegar chilled in the refrigerator.

❿

The flesh turns white after soaking in vinegar for two and a half hours.

❷

Slice off belly-bone.

❹

Sprinkle enough salt so you barely see the skin.

Take them out and drain vinegar on *bonzaru*.

⑪

❺

Flip and sprinkle lots of salt on flesh side as well.

Trace mark of spine and pluck small bones. Harder after flesh tightens.

⑫

⑬

Place belly side up in colander and cover with plastic wrap. Let rest in refrigerator overnight.

Iwashi
(sardine)

Scrape away innards and red muscle.

Cut off tail at root.

Insert thumb in belly and open fish to the tail.

Maiwashi, large-sized *iwashi* from Nagai, 200 g

Scrape off scales with tip of *debabocho* (broad-bladed kitchen knife).

Remove rib bones stuck in flesh as you carefully open it with your hands.

Pull up and raise spine and rib bones.

Cut off head diagonally from behind pectoral fin.

Pull spine and remove along with rib bones while trying not to damage flesh.

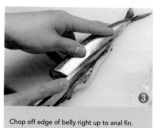

Chop off edge of belly right up to anal fin.

Slice off belly-bone.

Wipe red muscle away with cloth.

187

Sayori
(halfbeak)

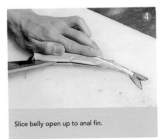

Slice belly open up to anal fin.

Trace flesh with finger and make sure there are no small bones left.

Sayori from Futtsu, 70 g

Remove innards.

Sprinkle salt lightly on both sides of sayori.

Scrape off scales with tip of debabocho (broad-bladed kitchen knife).

Insert knife along spine and slice open flesh.

Extract belly fin while pressing down with knife.

Slice off spine.

When flesh starts to sweat a little, rinse with water.

Cut off head behind pectoral fin.

Slice off belly-bone as well.

Drain on colander and put in refrigerator.

Kuruma Ebi

(prawn)

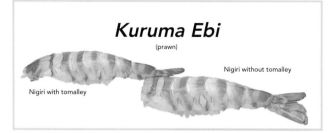

Nigiri without tomalley

Nigiri with tomalley

Live *kuruma ebi*, wild from Tokyo Bay, 50 g

Skewer from base of *ebi*'s legs.

Blanch by chilling quickly in ice water to stop color from turning further.

Skewer straight in between shell and flesh up to tail so tail won't bend.

Cook for three and a half to four minutes.

Avoid chilling flesh too much, take out when it's at around body temperature inside.

Boil salt water and put *ebi* in it.

Grab *ebi* and check to see if it's cooked through by feeling its bounciness.

Remove skewer, rotating it. Bring *ebi* to counter.

189

Sumi Ika

(squid)

Arrange flesh of mantle in colander, put plastic wrap on it and place in refrigerator.

Sumi ika from Nagasaki, 300 g

Peel outer skin.

Cut open root of tentacles and remove innards and ink sac.

Once water boils again, put them on colander.

Remove pen by pushing it forward.

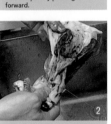

Cut into edge of mantle and from there, peel thin skin.

Massage tentacles, and when sliminess comes out, rinse with water.

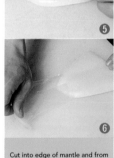

Open mantle and pull out tentacles.

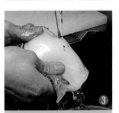

Cut into edge of mantle and from there, peel thin skin.

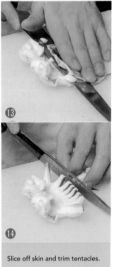

Cook in lightly salted boiling water.

Slice off skin and trim tentacles.

Rinse mantle with water and wash away squid ink.

Remove leftover skin with wet cloth.

Aori Ika

(bigfin reef squid)

Remove innards and take tentacles off mantle.

3

Aori ika from Sasebo, 2.4 kg

Remove fins and outer skin from mantle.

4

Slice fin in half.

7

Slice vertically in middle of mantle.

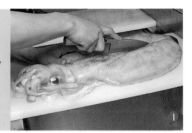

1

Slice mantle into four pieces vertically.

5

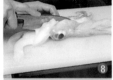

8

Cut open root of tentacles (head part). Carve out eyeballs and pull out and remove ink sac and innards.

Remove cartilage.

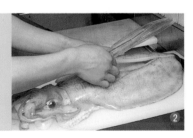

2

Peel thin skin with wet cloth. The fresher, the easier.

6

Boil water and deposit tentacles. After it boils again, let tentacles cook for a little less than a minute.

9

Koika

(small squid)

The same prepping method as *sumi ika*

Koika from Izumi in Kagoshima Prefecture, 50 g

Mantle of *warizuke* size. Peel thin skin just for what you'll use right away.

1

The tentacles are small, so boil them in water, not salted water.

2

Aka Gai
(surf clam)

Slice off gut attached to string.

Aka gai from Yuriage

Insert shucker from hinge.

Trim edge of strings.

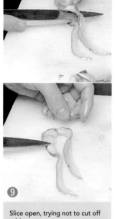

Slice open, trying not to cut off adductor.

With shucker, take off adductor attached to shell.

Cut open flesh horizontally.

Strip flesh.

Rinse thoroughly with water.

Slice off dark red innards.

Put them in colander and shake and wash with running water.

Rinse stripped flesh and slice off strings.

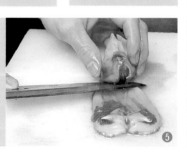

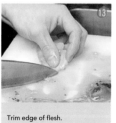

Trim edge of flesh.

Only five to six stripped in advance, the rest as orders come in.

192

Miru Gai

(geoduck clam)

From left: siphon, strings, adductor, umbo and innards.

⑥

Miru gai from Cape Irago

Open shell with shucker.

①

Peel off skin on siphon with shucker.

⑦

Scrape off remaining skin with tip of knife.

⑧

Take off adductor from shell and remove one side of shell.

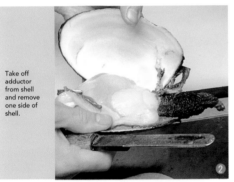

②

Slice open siphon.

⑨

Separate adductor from other shell so the flesh comes free.

③

④

Slice off membrane in siphon.

⑩

Rinse with water.

⑫

⑤

Slice and sort siphon, adductor, strings, and innards.

Cut off hard part of siphon at tip.

⑪

⑬

Six pieces' worth. Drain water and put in *tane* box.

193

Anago
(conger eel)

Anago from Nojima, 120 to 130 g

Firmly press down flesh with left hand following knife's movement, and cut open to tip of tail.

Remove innards. Because it's fresh, comes out in one go.

Insert knife under spine and slice off.

① Placing *anago* with back facing you, pierce *meuchi* (rod) above pectoral fin to stabilize.

Draw knife on flesh to remove muck.

Draw knife on flesh again to flatten.

② Insert *debabocho* (broad-bladed kitchen knife) right behind pectoral fin.

Cut off tail and dorsal fin.

Cut head off right behind pectoral fin.

③ Slide knife along spine and open back.

Remove sinews attached to flesh as well.

Rinse well with water and get rid of sliminess.

To avoid having *anago* dance around, use an *otoshibuta* (drop-lid).

Change water and massage while washing. Repeat three times.

Simmer over medium heat. Remove foam that starts to float up.

Once it starts to boil, put *anago* in it.

Heat pot with plenty of water and put white granulated sugar in it.

Add *mirin* (sweet rice wine).

Each *anago* makes three to pieces of nigiri and is ready after twenty-five minutes.

Add *shoyu* (soy sauce).

The flesh is too soft to be picked up by *saibashi* (long chopsticks), so scoop with wooden spoon.

Arrange flesh-side up on tray, cover with wet cloth, and store at room temperature.

195

Tako
(octopus)

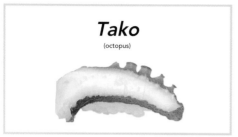

Madako, Sajima, 1.5 kg

The innards inside the head are removed in the morning at the market, but the remaining flesh moves around vigorously.

Insert knife by eyes at root of head and carve them out.

The live *tako* starts to go limp.

Previously limp, it swells a little now.

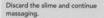

Discard the slime and continue massaging.

Keep massaging away. Don't wash yet because the skin will come off.

In washing tub, start massaging as is.

Massage with your whole weight. It will feel slimy after ten minutes or so.

The sliminess begins to abate. You can also massage it more easily now.

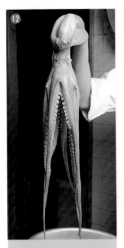

After massaging thoroughly to tip of tentacles for 30-40 minutes, sliminess finally goes away.

Continue massaging, and they slope back a little. Done.

Until tentacles curl outward, dunk in and out of hot water a couple of times.

Once tentacles are curled up, sink body in hot water and boil it.

Boil over high heat for sixteen minutes. Broth said to be effective for chilblains.

When the tentacles bow out as if squaring shoulders, you're almost done massaging.

Bring a lot of water to boil, and hang tako from a wire and submerge from tip of tentacles.

Don't touch with hands or its skin will peel. Hook wire on head, pull out of pot, and let hang.

Chill at room temperature like so until it's at body temperature.

197

Hamaguri
(hard clam)

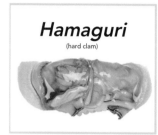

Place in boiling water and return to a boil.

Pick up with fingers and push out gut.

Stripped flesh of *hamaguri* from Ise,
80 to 90 g per with shell

Lay on colander to cool.
Cook to core with the residual heat.

Remove all sinew as well.

Skewer siphons of *hamaguri* with bamboo stick.

Insert knife from leg and open flesh horizontally.

In running water, hold and spin bamboo
skewer to wash stripped flesh.

Hamazume reduction sauce: add sugar, *shoyu*
(soy sauce), and *mirin* (sweet rice wine) to broth
from boiling *hamaguri* and simmer down.

Pile and arrange open *hamaguri* and pour
hamazume over them.

After removing sand and sliminess, lay on
colander to drain.

Cover with wet cloth to avoid drying and let rest.

Shako
(mantis shrimp)

Once boiling, skim the foam.

Flip and let *hamazume* penetrate all the way through.

Shako with eggs from Koshiba

Flip them twice or so. The juice also comes out, and it marinates better.

Put *shako* in it.

Boil water and add white granulated sugar.

After returning to a boil, skim the foam and turn off heat.

Good to eat after a few hours of marinating.

Add *mirin* (sweet rice wine) for a better after-taste than sake.

Add *shoyu* (soy sauce) and boil to reduce alcohol content.

Cool to room temperature in broth. When completely cooled, take out of broth, and they're done.

Awabi

(abalone)

Awabi, female from Iwawada, 800 g

Insert handle of grater between shell and flesh and take off adductor.

1

Pull out flesh, and forcefully use hand like blade to pry off.

2 **3**

Pull out membrane and gut from shell. Simmer gut and make hors d'oeuvres with it.

4

Cut off membrane attached to shell.

5

Remove shell muscle by threshing with base of knife.

6

Scrub flesh with *tawashi* (scourer) and get rid of dirt and sliminess.

7

Wash away dirt thoroughly on front and in the folds.

8

Put *awabi* in pot with water, add less sake than the amount of water, and cook over high heat.

9

Skim the foam when it starts to boil.

10

Reduce heat and keep adding water and skimming foam.

11

Simmer for three to four hours. Done when flesh turns amber-colored.

12

Let cool in broth. The soft ones for nigiri, the harder ones become hors d'oeuvre.

13

Ikura
(salmon roe)

Raw *ikura* from Sanriku. Select ones with soft skin by tasting.

Massage and unravel *ikura* after placing in water.

Put in colander and drain in refrigerator.

Break the thin outer skin of the skein.

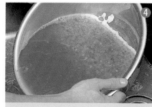

Wash away dirt and scraps of skin.

Add water, hot water, and salt, and continue to massage and unravel it.

Marinate in mixture of sake, *shoyu*, and salt that has been boiled and chilled.

Put salt into warm water (slightly hotter than bath).

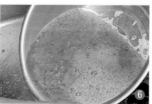

Remove squashed scraps and hard roe. Repeat until clean.

Taste after a few hours and add more marinade if necessary.

201

Tamagoyaki
(Japanese omelette)

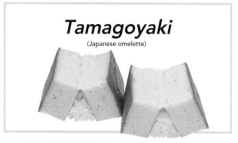

Using two eggs at a time, add in and grind. Repeat.

Eggs, *shiba ebi* (from Mikawa), *yamatoimo* (Japanese mountain yam), sugar, salt, and *mirin*.

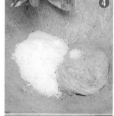

Purée peeled *shiba ebi*.

Add pinch of salt and sugar and keep grinding well.

Place in a mortar, and add grated *yamatoimo*.

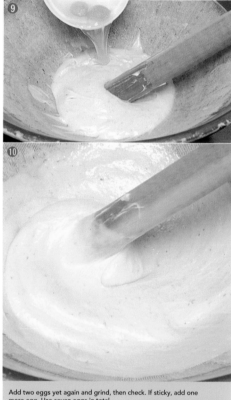

Add two eggs yet again and grind, then check. If sticky, add one more egg. Use seven eggs in total.

When it gets stickier, adjust with *mirin*.

Grind well with pestle.

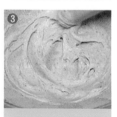

Heat omelette maker or pan and oil.

Measure by putting pan close to face. Try not to heat too much.

x

202

Pour egg mixture into pan. Shake and flatten, avoiding air bubbles.

It starts to rise after twenty minutes. Insert metal skewers along the edges of the pan.

Put wooden lid on *tamagoyaki* and press down hard to get rid of bubbles.

When *tamagoyaki* swells further, twist metal skewer into edge.

Fill right up to brim and place over minimum heat.

Thirty minutes...

Flip pan upside down and catch *tamagoyaki* with wooden lid.

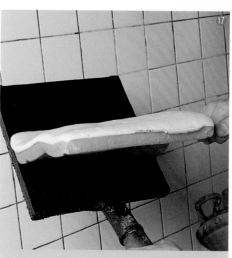

Insert two *saibashi* (long chopsticks) between *tamagoyaki* and pan, lift up *tamagoyaki*, and flip.

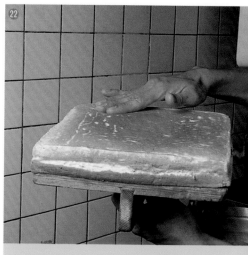

Touch with belly of your fingers to make sure it's cooked through.

Put pan with flipped *tamagoyaki* back over slightly higher heat.

Let cool on *bonzaru* (wicker colander).

Tamagoyaki done. The side grilled first is the front.

203

Nitsume
(reduction sauce)

Completely fill pot with water and add white granulated sugar.

After it reaches a boil, skim foam. Reduce heat to low after tasting.

On the next day, pour into smaller pot and put over minimum heat after adding *mirin* (sweet rice wine).

After twelve hours, it's reduced to a quarter; after seventeen, to an eighth.

Strain *anago* (conger eel) broth.

Simmer down by half—on a low flame, uncovered, from morning to evening.

Cool finished *nitsume*, put in jar, and store in refrigerator.

Nikiri
(thin and sweet glaze)

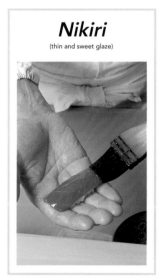

Pour sake and *shoyu* (soy sauce) in pot, add a little *mirin* (sweet rice wine), and heat.

When it starts to boil, flambé it and reduce.

Let cool and it's done.

Pour into small bowl and bring to counter.

Except for the small *shinko* (young gizzard shad), where we use two to three per piece of nigiri, we twist the tail of *kohada* (gizzard shad) a little bit to the left to express its liveliness. And when a customer with keen eyes compliments, "What a magnificent shape and form," I feel excited and rewarded as a craftsman.

But no matter how good it looks, it has to taste good. If I could theorize this, the visual feast of the varying hues of silver-skinned fish, whitefish, colored fish, lean meat, and simmered items, along with the oral feast of their distinct flavors and differences in aroma, is the ultimate characteristic of *Edomae*-style nigiri.

So as I already told you, for instance, the degree of seasoning, how much you pickle the *kohada,* has to be adjusted according to its size and quality. When chefs skimp on that prepping process, *kohada* becomes a regular *tane* in *nami* sushi (the most affordable assortment) rather than the King of Nigiri that it should be.

I share all of our preparing process because I think the delight of nigiri doubles if you understand how we work: "Ah I see, this *katsuo* (bonito) tastes better because he smokes it with straw fire," or "The adductor of the *aka gai* (surf clam) is sliced at the same thickness as the strings. That's why it looks beautiful as nigiri."

I'm sure some people are feeling nervous and wondering, "Are you sure you want to disclose all these secrets?"

You see, the taste of sushi hinges on the last leg you put out in the prepping process, that "one step over a thousand leagues." Even if you reenact our whole prepping process, disclosed thoroughly here, it wouldn't be possible to recreate the exact same taste. I'm convinced of this, actually.

—Jiro

Chapter 4

Nori Maki, Tamagoyaki

JIRO SUSHI TALK 4

NORI MAKI, TAMAGOYAKI

"To tell you the truth, I am the unworthy disciple of a master who invented the hand roll."

There is a masterpiece called *Sushitsu* (Sushi Connoisseur) that was published in 1930. Its mysterious author, Ganosuke Nagase, must have been an educated idler who paid out of his own pocket to enjoy *Edomae*-style nigiri to his heart's content. He wrote, "When you roast *nori* well, as you would *unagi* (eel), with *bincho* charcoal, it's wonderful without losing its aroma or flavor, but there is no sushi restaurant nowadays that practices this."

In the present day in the Heisei period, Jiro Ono practices this.

Nori
The character of *nori* (dried seaweed) is determined by how you roast it

Nori is such an important ingredient that it can affect the impression of a sushi restaurant itself. Most customers order *nori maki* (roll wrapped in dried seaweed) after eating nigiri to round out the meal. If, at that point, the *nori* tastes fishy or can't be chewed off because it's stale, then all the guest's feeling of satisfaction will vanish.

This is why, every morning at our restaurant, we roast the amount we use per day with *kishu bincho* charcoal (originated by a merchant called Bincho from Kishu).

We use *bincho* charcoal because, with ordinary charcoal, the flame rises so high that it burns the *nori*. We can't use gas because it emits moisture, nor an electric range because it has weak heating power. If we used an electric range to roast our day's worth of *nori*, it'd probably take an hour. However, with *bincho* charcoal, it only takes fifteen minutes. Plus, it remains crispy even in the evening, and as soon as you put it in your mouth, it melts.

As you know, the heating power of *bincho* charcoal is extremely intense, so even though the flame doesn't blaze up, if you don't pay attention the fire spreads right away.

So I often tell my son, who recently started to work on this part of the prep, "Roast it as if you're slapping it on the gridiron of the cook stove, and don't sweep the gridiron with it."

You can't roast delicious *nori* unless you put the flame on it instantaneously at an almost perpendicular angle, then quickly flip it front and back with *tekaeshi* (a technique typically used for turning over nigiri). If you roast it horizontally as if you're sweeping with a broom, then the heat doesn't distribute evenly, and there will be a part that's burnt. However, this *tekaeshi* is considered difficult for beginners. Me, I've roasted *nori* every morning for over forty years since I became an apprentice at Kyobashi, and it's just a matter of getting used to it. Once you get used to it, it's no big deal.

At any rate, the character of *nori* is determined by how you roast it. You can't roast it a hundred percent. If you try to roast it one hundred percent, it burns, so be ready to stop roasting at ninety-five, and equally heat all four corners. Then the color turns vivid beyond recognition and an aroma of the ocean beyond description rises in the air.

The season for *nori* is winter. In Tokyo Bay back in the day, they were able to catch young seaweed in December that looked as if lacquer were poured into the ocean. However, we can't even wish for *nori* like that now.

That's because they grow *nori* buds differently than in the past. Until the Tokyo Bay fishermen surrendered their fishing rights in 1962, they used to stick bamboo and brushwood to gather laver in the shallow tideland, and they attached buds there. The buds were underwater and grew at high tide, but at low tide they were exposed to the air and dried out. Ebb and flow. And through this repetition, good buds grew.

In the harvesting season, they picked the ones that were ready to eat, and made them into *nori* and dried them under the sun. This is how they became roasted *nori* as aromatic and fluffy as a thick Persian rug, and it melted in the mouth.

Lately, however, fishermen float nets with buds deep offshore. This way, the buds soak in seawater all year round, so they grow faster. They reap with a machine that looks like a relative of a vacuum cleaner, and they dry everything electrically, thick and thin all at once, on a belt conveyer. Because they make it this way, the finished product is flat and inconsistently roasted. It doesn't melt when you put it in your mouth.

But I run a sushi restaurant. I can't just indulge in nostalgia. As a sushi chef, my obligation is to roast *nori* as well as I can in the present day. The only way to bring back the aroma, sweetness, and texture from the good old days is to make it crispy by heating it with *bincho* charcoal.

I trust my *nori* salesperson, a pro among pros, and it seems that most of ours comes from the Ariake Sea in Saga. In fact, a regular complimented me a couple of days ago, saying, "You use such nice *nori* at your restaurant." He is actually the president of a famous *nori* wholesaler. We received an endorsement from an authority.

Gunkan Maki: Ikura
It's become possible for us to serve delicious *ikura* (salmon roe) all year round

Because demand has increased, fishermen have started to land *sake* (salmon) with spawn directly at Choshi Harbor. The freshness is exceptional compared to the time they transported it to Tsukiji via Hokkaido.

However, lately, for some reason, *akizake* (autumn salmon) ascend earlier, and the season for *ikura* keeps moving up. Up until very recently, we couldn't eat delicious *ikura* unless it was November, but in 1996 they started to appear in early September, and by mid-October the roe were already hard.

Until 1995, September spawns were premature.

But in 1997, *akizake* with scant roe started to appear in August after the *obon* festival, and by the end of the month the flavor was plenty developed. At this rate, by October all the roe will be too hard.

Ikura's asset is the grains' tenderness. Roe that seems to pop in the mouth, the skin melting, comes from salmon caught offshore. They return to the river where they were born and grew up to spawn, but as they get closer to the mouth of the river, the eggs get hard like ping-pong balls. This is why *ikura* obtained offshore is the only option.

The timing on shore is also crucial. The skin gets hard when it's exposed to air for too long. I have to head out early so I'm there when the salmon fishmonger slits the fish's stomach at seven in the morning.

You can tell with your hands whether they're hard or soft. But when you come across the ones that seem good, then to be extra careful, pluck a grain and test the quality by putting it in your mouth. The roe's firmness is consistent in each egg sac, so once you taste one or two, you'll know.

Ikura is our newest *neta*. We started serving it thanks to the words of a longtime regular whom I can't hold a candle to.

This was about fifteen to sixteen years ago. He showed up holding tupperware filled with *ikura* and said, "I just came back from a business trip to Hokkaido and found extraordinarily delicious raw *ikura* there. Maybe because they marinate it in *shoyu* (soy sauce) and *mirin* (sweet rice wine), it doesn't have the same fishiness as the salted *ikura* sold in Tokyo. When I put it on warm rice, it stimulates my appetite, and I can keep on filling my bowl. And I ask you this because I know I can count on you: Can you make even more delicious *ikura*? I want to bring it home and have it as a side for dinner."

At Nijyo Market in Sapporo, they marinate raw *ikura* in *shoyu* (soy sauce) on the spot. I'd heard it was really popular with tourists, but it was my first time seeing it in person. When I tried it, indeed, there was no fishiness to it whatsoever. It made sense that someone like him who appreciated great flavors would fall in love with it.

Unfortunately, he has since passed away, but this guest was a benefactor who treated me kindly every chance he got. I mustn't turn down someone like him, I thought, and started studying about *ikura* right away. I couldn't help but feel inspired.

Soon after, I perfected the flavor to his satisfaction, and he was overjoyed that he could have my *ikura* at his dinner table.

So the beginning of our *shoyu*-marinated *ikura* was for a regular and not as nigiri *neta*.

One day, however, I thought: If someone who appreciates good flavors as much as he does is happy with it, then other guests will welcome it as well. So I served it in a small bowl as a sake side, and it was received even better than I expected. And I felt so great about it, I started serving *gunkan maki* ("warship roll": nigiri wrapped in *nori* with the *neta* on top). In Tokyo back then, sushi restaurants that served raw *ikura* were rare. Perhaps we were the only one.

But raw *ikura* has a drawback. We can only use it for about two and a half months in autumn. The time we can serve it is too short.

As I thought about it, I had an epiphany. *Right, I should just freeze it.* Freeze it, and even that regular would be enjoying delicious *ikura* rice all year round.

So I put a whole skein of raw eggs in what was at the time a state-of-the-art freezer at minus ten degrees (Celsius) but failed miserably. When I defrosted it, the skin ripped and the liquid inside came out, and we couldn't use it at all. Then I tried freezing it after dismantling it. But it didn't defrost well that way either.

So I visited a delicacy store in Tsukiji that handled salted dried goods and asked, "I keep failing at freezing it in this and that way, why do you think?"

And the head guy answered, "It's not only raw *ikura* that's challenging to freeze. Even with *kazunoko* (herring roe), it becomes crumpled, and after some time, it separates. But if you flavor it, it'll be okay. The salted *ikura* that's in our freezer—the quality doesn't change even after one year."

The key was the salt content. After I returned to my restaurant and marinated the roe in *shoyu*, froze it, and defrosted it, both the flavor and the appearance stayed the way it was when it was raw.

But the problem was the minus-ten-degrees freezer. When I defrosted a batch that had been frozen for about a month, the roe just washed away. I had no idea why. I'd heard that frozen *maguro* (tuna) didn't change color after being frozen for many years. I wondered how they quality-controlled *maguro*. So this time I went to ask the *maguro* fishmongers. They informed me that they froze it with a minus-fifty-degrees deep freezer that was state-of-the-art at the time.

From there, I went straight to buy this state-of-the-art minus-fifty-degrees deep freezer, since I wanted to serve frozen *ikura* with the exact same taste as raw *ikura*. And when they're frozen in a deep freezer, as the *maguro* fishmongers president said, *ikura* doesn't change a thing even after a few months.

A -50° C freezer, originally acquired to serve *shoyu*-marinated raw *ikura* all year round. Frozen in small batches.

However, when you defrost it, the *ikura* goes weird. And the days of trial and error continued, and I finally came up with a rational defrosting method in the following season.

This is how I do it.

When defrosting, first transfer *ikura* from the minus-fifty-degrees deep freezer to a minus-ten-degrees freezer. Then after a while, put it in a refrigerator until it's restored completely to a raw state. This is how we can serve delicious *ikura* all year round.

Of course, some customers who see how *ikura* is always displayed in our *neta* box might say, "Authentic sushi restaurants should adhere to what's in season. It's not acceptable to use frozen ingredients."

They're right for sure, but back then, when I was trying to come up with the successful method for about two years, all I thought about was how to serve *ikura* all year round, and seasonality was nowhere on my mind. I wonder how much *ikura* I tasted back then. I put so many ingredients like *tako* (octopus) and *awabi* (abalone) in my stomach until I settled on their flavors. I'm sure I had very many skeins of *ikura*.

Judging from the number of orders we receive, most people must feel, "What tastes good tastes good." I have my customers' support, I believe.

By the way, the *shoyu*-marinated *ikura* that I made for my regular was for bowls of rice, so I made it strong in flavor, but ever since I started using it for *gunkan maki*, I cut back on the salt content. The *shari* (vinegared rice) has saltiness as well. The tongue feels more stimulation from straight salt, even though *shoyu* contains it, so we tend to flavor our *ikura* with the *shoyu*.

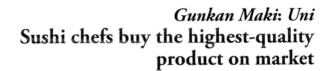

Gunkan Maki: Uni
Sushi chefs buy the highest-quality product on market

Many say, "The season for *uni* (sea urchin) is summer," but in Tokyo, *uni* tastes better in the colder months.

In Hokkaido, the home of *uni*, it's in season in summer on the west side in the Sea of Japan, and in winter, on the east side in the Pacific Ocean. So almost all year round they can catch *uni* that's good to eat, but the "white" kind that I use (*ezo murasaki uni*/purple sea urchin) is vulnerable to heat, so especially in summer it melts fast. Even when it's flown in by jet, by the evening, the flesh starts to ooze out.

In the summertime, I also make nigiri with "red" (*ezo bafun uni*/short-spined sea urchin). This *uni* is a rare and expensive product, but its bits are harder, so it's not the best suited for our nigiri. I ate and compared them and came to this conclusion, so I try to use the white.

Anyhow, each bit of the white is the size of an adult's thumb; first-time customers are surprised. More than anything, the sophisticated sweetness, aroma, and coloring match perfectly with our *shari* (vinegared rice).

All the raw *uni* in Tsukiji come from the north. The small *uni* from western Japan never make it there. They don't taste bad for sure. They deserve to be called "the best *uni* in Japan," as people from Yamaguchi Prefecture brag. However, they can't catch enough to transport to Tokyo, and it also probably doesn't last long enough. From the west, they send *tsubu uni* (grainy sea urchin) soaked in alcohol or salt.

By the way, someone who lives in Yamaguchi Prefecture sent me raw *uni* from Kudamatsu (Seto Inland Sea), but when I tried it, the smell of the cedar from the box had permeated the *uni*. The odor bothered me, and a hint of bitterness had also rubbed off. It was unfortunate since they'd sent me supreme-quality *uni*.

In that respect, they are advanced in Hokkaido and use wooden boxes without any aroma. Before that, they put a sheet of deodorizer in the box. They give it such detailed attention.

At any rate, when it comes to *uni*, Hokkaido and Tsukiji have a long relationship. Now they use jet planes, but in 1969, they used night trains. When I went to the shore in the morning, many men were carrying boxes of *uni* on their backs.

When I asked "Where are you from," they answered "Hokkaido."

All the people who transported *uni* were former National Railways workers. I don't know how it is now, but the retirees from National Railways owned a rail pass that they could use to go anywhere for free.

From Hokkaido to Tokyo must have taken all day at the time. They didn't yet have any coolers made out of styrofoam, so if they slacked off, then the freshness went away. But they worked out a way to supply *uni* without getting complaints.

The deodorizing sheets and odor-free wooden boxes are the fruit of their efforts.

The *uni* I use is a brand called Hadate from Hakodate, and because they grow near the four northern islands that aren't fished excessively, the pieces are surprisingly fat. There are four ranks—gold, green, blue, and navy—according to the colored labels, but they're all wonderful to the point you can call all of them specialty products.

At Tsukiji, they sell *uni* including imported ones in dozens of different levels of rankings. By the way, when I researched the wholesale price one day, there was a huge spread, from 300 yen per box to 15,000 yen per box. The quality runs the whole gamut, and, of course, Hadate is there at the top.

What makes it the best is that there are five pieces of *uni* from one shell. You have to wash the dirt away with salt water and get rid of the shell particles, and then tighten the flesh and then ship, and if an experienced person doesn't work on this process, more often than not, the edges of the *uni* pieces crumble.

Excluding the crumbled *uni*, and strictly selecting by size, form, color, and sheen, they only place pieces that are up to standard in the gold and green boxes.

So the gold is a very rare, valuable product. That's because they don't give the gold stamp unless the *uni* miraculously fulfills and scores perfect points on three criteria: a viscous grain density; plump veins, indicative of freshness; and a spotless, bright yellow color.

Such superb *uni* is found to complete only one out of five hundred boxes. Even someone like me who buys *uni* every day only sees it maybe four or five times per season. In 1996 and 1997, I didn't see it once. Of course if I do, I definitely buy it, but whoever gets to taste it is extremely lucky. Generally speaking, the green that we use all the time is the best-quality product on the market. The difference between the gold and the green is so subtle that I can't really tell them apart, to be honest.

I roll *uni* as *gunkan maki* ("warship roll": nigiri wrapped in *nori* with the *neta* on top). As you can tell from its name, *gunkan maki* isn't a recent invention. When I became a sushi craftsman in 1951, they were already serving it at Kyobashi Restaurant. I don't remember seeing *ikura* as *neta*, but they used to make *gunkan maki* with *uni* and even *kobashira* (small scallops). If I think about the transportation capacity, there was no way they could transport it from Hokkaido, so they were probably using local *uni*. *Uni* from Hayama (Sagami Bay) was famous. Although we can't get ahold of enough, they are sometimes caught in Tokyo Bay or Sagami Bay even now.

Some have a harsh opinion: "It's nigiri because you *nigiru* (a Japanese verb meaning 'grip' or 'clasp'). *Gunkan maki* is not nigiri."

However, I *nigiru* even the *shari* (vinegared rice) in *gunkan*. If I don't, the *shari* doesn't form itself. So it's beyond me why anyone would say, "*Gunkan maki* is not nigiri."

It's certain that there is an issue. There are customers who don't have it right away after I roll the *uni* into *gunkan*. Since we use body temperature *shari*, if the customer yaps away as the *gunkan* sits on the counter, the *uni* starts to melt. In extreme cases, the *shari* becomes soggy and the *nori* hard to chew off because of the humidity.

It's the same for any nigiri, but especially with *gunkan maki* and *maki* (roll) items, I'm in trouble if the customers don't have them right after I serve them. So I think I understand the feeling of people who say, "I don't like *gunkan*." But those sushi lovers who "have them as I serve them" appreciate it because *uni* and *nori* taste good together. With *nori* that we roast with *bincho* charcoal every morning, even if we roll it as *gunkan*, it doesn't remain in the mouth. However, there is a regular who orders saying, "No, no, you say so, but please make nigiri with it and not roll it as *gunkan*." I asked why, to which he answered, "*Uni* is the softest of nigiri-*dane*. So when you roll it as *gunkan*, the harder *nori* overwhelms the *uni*. Even if you roast it with *bincho* charcoal, the fiber of *nori* remains in the mouth. But if it's only the *tane* and *shari*, then nothing remains in the mouth."

This is the guest's conviction, so I shut up and make a nigiri.

Of course, I can make nigiri with *uni*. Grab *shari* and adjust the form, and after putting the *neta* on it, adjust it again. Unless it's good-quality *uni*, the pieces collapse, but Hadate is firm enough.

Many regulars have it as a side, I assume because the rich and sensitive flavor and texture of raw *uni* go well with sake. Raw *uni* alone doesn't satisfy them, so there are regulars who place complicated orders. For instance, "Put thinly sliced *ika* (squid) and *uni* in a small bowl and drizzle a little bit of wasabi *joyu* (soy sauce with wasabi)." According to that particular old face, "When the plain *ika*, the rich *uni*, and the spicy wasabi meet, the umami triples. It goes well with sake."

Tai (sea bream) and *hirame* (flounder) are served at ordinary restaurants, but if you want to eat delicious *uni*, become a regular at a good sushi place. It's sushi chefs who buy the market's highest-quality product of the day.

Even if the price hikes up, we want to serve good *uni*. As with *hon maguro* (bluefin tuna), we use *uni* as a matter of pride as craftsmen.

Nori Maki
I make *sumaki* (roll wrapped with a bamboo mat) and *temaki* (roll wrapped with hands) according to the customer's preference

Nori maki (*kanpyo maki*/dried gourd roll) is profound: "mere *kanpyo maki*, mighty *kanpyo maki*." First off, even housewives make it, so *kanpyo maki* doesn't become an attraction for a sushi restaurant unless there is a clear difference in flavor between amateurs and professionals. It's one of the *neta* that keeps me on my toes.

This is why we put in unrelenting effort even for just boiling it. We divide

After the lunch service, the entire staff gets together for their meal, made from each day's leftover *tane*. On this occasion, excess vinegared rice was steamed and topped with lean meat as *tekka don*, and *chutoro* that had changed color was stewed with ginger.

2-kg *kanpyo* in five parts and boil 400 grams per batch. Cut the *kanpyo* in the length of a whole *nori maki* and soak it in water for one day. When it gets soft, sprinkle it with salt and massage it thoroughly to remove the harshness. And the next step is scalding. After scalding, you select the pieces. We check carefully and remove the hard part once and for all. If I find a wide part, then I split it into smaller pieces. Lastly, we flavor it by simmering.

So to finish just the *kanpyo*, it takes two days.

The crucial point in making delicious *kanpyo maki* is the selection process. It's a bother to feel any toughness and discomfort when you put it in your mouth. So we make all the pieces the same soft consistency. If we don't, it doesn't become the "*Yokozuna* of *Makimono* (the sumo champ of rolled items)."

We don't waste the hard parts that we don't serve to our customers. We simmer them in a separate batch from the soft ones, dice them small, and use them as one of the toppings for *chirashi-zushi* (variety of toppings, mainly seafood, on a bed of rice) that we have in our kitchen. It's really good when we mix in *geso* (squid tentacles).

Young people nowadays don't know the true pleasure of *kanpyo maki*. They seem to prefer *negitoro maki* (tuna and chives roll), *natto maki* (fermented soybean roll), and avocado rolls, but I can't possibly agree that they taste good. When I act as a customer of Sukiyabashi Jiro and have *makimono*, first I order *nori maki* (*kanpyo maki*) or *anago maki* (conger eel roll). Whether or not I want cucumber in the latter depends on how I'm feeling that day. I ask the chef to brush a little bit of *nitsume* (reduction sauce) on the surface if it's *anago maki*. Sometimes there are orders requesting wasabi, but our *anago* goes better with *nitsume* than with wasabi and *nikiri shoyu* (thin and sweet soy sauce glaze).

However, there aren't many customers who know that we can also roll *anago*, and I have no intention of advertising it as being delicious.

If its popularity increases, we won't have much *tekuzu* (sliced edges) left. And if that happens, I'll feel bad for our young guys. After we close, they make rolls and nigiri with leftover *anago*. I don't want to take away this feast from them.

There is one more *makimono* that's not so well known: *oboro maki* (ground and cooked fish roll). There are passionate fans of this. Our *oboro* is made with *shiba ebi* (shiba shrimp) and *kuruma ebi* (prawn) that's been used as a display in the *tane* box, so there is enough umami in it. There is no coarse texture or discomfort when you put it in your mouth. Even the color is a beautiful natural pink. According to a regular who is a fan, "I don't like sweet things, but your *oboro* is an exception. The soft and sophisticated sweetness and smooth texture go perfectly well with the *nori*'s aroma and the amount of vinegar in the rice."

So he always orders *oboro maki* to finish his meal.

Typically, sushi chefs make *oboro* with white meat. They drain the fat off boiled whitefish by massaging it under running water, and then grind it with a mortar, so only its fiber becomes *oboro*. Depending on the management policy of the restaurant, this is sufficient. The chefs don't feel the need to overstretch and use *shiba ebi*.

So for our young guys who go back to their hometowns, I teach them tricks for making *oboro* with white meat. If you use whitefish, you naturally end up with *nakaochi* (leftover flesh on the spine). You store that in the refrigerator, and once there is enough, you can make *oboro*.

For *nori maki*, unless the larger hand-rolled variety is requested, we use *makisu* (a bamboo mat for rolling). Well, it's not like I have a stubborn belief that "*temaki* (hand roll) is not nigiri." I simply roll how sushi chefs traditionally have for a long time: *kanpyo maki* taste the best cut in four pieces; six for *kyuri maki* (cucumber roll), *oboro maki*, and *tekka maki* (tuna roll). I think so after trying and comparing.

When I make a roll with my hands, the *nori* remains crispy. And the aroma of the ocean is fragrant. However, it can be too fragrant, overwhelming the flavor of the core ingredient. So I understand the feeling of people who avoid *temaki*.

There is another issue with *temaki*. You have to keep holding it with your hands until you're done, and if you aren't quick, the *nori* becomes hard to chew off because it gets soggy. By contrast, with *sumaki* (roll wrapped with a bamboo mat) the taste doesn't deteriorate as soon.

But it's questionable to decide arbitrarily that "*temaki* is bad no matter what." There is no need to criticize and attack people who want to enjoy the aroma and crisp texture of *nori*. I personally don't feel that it's wrong and don't go intoning, "Pardon me, dear guest, but *temaki* is not nigiri."

If there is a request, I make a roll with my hands. This is simply a matter of customer preference.

However, I think there are *neta* that do well or don't in *temaki* form. *Takuan* (pickled radish) doesn't. *Kanpyo* is definitely better rolled with a *makisu*. *Anago*, too. *Anakyu* with *anago* and *kyuri* (cucumber) also. As for *oboro*, it tastes good to roll with *makisu*, hundred percent. If anything, I'd have *tekka maki* (tuna rolls) as *temaki*. In particular, very rich *otoro* (fatty tuna) tastes great as *temaki*.

Apparently, the person who invented *temaki* was the sushi master from Kyobashi Restaurant. A regular saw him making *temaki* for himself—giving it a twirl with his hands and eating it when he was hungry. And the guest said, "Roll one for me, too." When that was well received, the boss started serving it to the general public. I heard a story like that. To tell you the truth, I am the unworthy disciple of a master who was "the inventor of *temaki*."

Tamagoyaki
Half *shiba ebi* (shiba shrimp) and half eggs. We cook it for an hour.

I make traditional Tokyo-style *tamagoyaki* (Japanese omelette) the way I learned during my apprenticeship. But I improved it a little bit, so ours is moister. That's because I dramatically increased the amount of *shiba ebi* (shiba shrimp). Years ago Kyobashi Restaurant put 230 grams of *shiba* per sheet of *tamagoyaki*, but ours has 400 grams. We use half *shiba ebi* and half eggs.

They say they mostly used ground whitefish at sushi restaurants back then. But no matter how good the minced flesh is, there is still fishiness to it. However, *shiba* doesn't have that odor. And also because the flesh is soft, the *tamagoyaki* comes out soft and fluffy.

Lately, *shiba* catches from the seas around Japan have been poor. Sometimes they limit the amount you can buy, and at such times we use *komaki* (small *kuruma ebi*/prawn). Then the *tamagoyaki* comes out with such a beautiful color that the lack of *shiba ebi* is almost not an issue. However, the thing with *komaki* is that it stiffens once it's heated, so the *tamagoyaki* inevitably gets hard. That's the drawback.

No, it doesn't taste bad. *Komaki* doesn't. Its aroma is actually better than *shiba*'s. But the distinct feature of *tamagoyaki* is its fluffiness, so if possible, I want to continue using *shiba* that gives a soft finish. That's my thinking.

It takes an hour to cook one sheet of our *tamagoyaki*. There is a way to cook it faster. But you'd have to flip it while the inside was still too soft and might ruin it through carelessness. My son whom I have come to trust to cook *tamagoyaki* seems to spend a lot of time letting the heat reach the core.

Me, I could cook it much faster. But if I did absolutely everything then my work wouldn't be passed along to the next generation. That's why I decided to just watch without saying anything.

It's the same for any *neta*, but we flavor *tamagoyaki* to taste good atop *shari*. But recently, ninety percent of our customers eat it on its own and not as nigiri. In the past, we all made nigiri with it saddled on *shari* (vinegared rice).

If there isn't that vinegared aroma from the bottom, then the true flavor of *tamagoyaki* doesn't come out. Of course, it also tastes good rolled. When it's rolled, you can also taste the true flavor. When it's paired with vinegared rice or *nori*, the flavor comes out from the synergy.

Gari, Agari
Cleanse with *gari* (pickled ginger) and wash with powdered tea—that's the *Edomae* way

Gari (pickled ginger) tastes good in the season of young *shoga* (ginger), in spring. From April to May, the young *oumi shoga* (ginger from Oumi) starts to appear first in Kochi and then in Wakayama. Young *shoga* like this turns pale pink just by going through vinegar, and it's refreshing: "Ahhh, the height of spring!" Plus, it has a mild spiciness, so the amount that our customers have increases dramatically. In August, the pink color disappears, but our *gari* is always young *shoga*; we never use hard and spicy *hineshoga* (old ginger). That's because they dig a cave in the hillside and store young ginger that was just harvested, and probably because the temperature is cold and consistent, it doesn't age. So our *gari*'s flavor doesn't change throughout the year. Lately, new potatoes also start to appear in February or March. These were also stored in a cave the previous year.

Of course, we pickle our *gari* at our restaurant, using vinegar, salt, and white granulated sugar. The reason the sourness is slightly strong is that it's made to match the flavors of our nigiri. Commercial *gari* is too sweet and not edible. Saccharin usage is prohibited so that can't be it, but it's not the sweetness of sugar, either. I wonder what kind of sweetener they're using.

To enjoy delicious nigiri, you eliminate the flavor, fat, and aroma of the one you just had with the spiciness of *gari*, and then wash the inside of your mouth with a very hot *agari* (green tea for eating sushi) that's made with powdered tea. That's the *Edomae* way.

Sencha (classic unshaded green tea), which is delicious at a lukewarm temperature, surely has a nice flavor and aroma, but the tepidness can bring out the fishiness. *Agari* has to be hot.

This is why an apprentice boy at a sushi restaurant keeps an eye on how fast the guests are sipping it, and if a cup is becoming empty, it's refilled immediately. Using regular tea leaves would take too much time. If you make green tea by pouring hot water on expensive *shincha* (new tea) or *gyokuro* ("jade dew," the finest of Japanese teas), it doesn't taste good at all. This is why they came to use powdered tea, which turns into strong tea as soon as we pour hot water. Our powdered tea is from Kawane in Shizuoka Prefecture, and we get a direct shipment from the local producers.

It's hard to make a sushi restaurant's *agari*. It's not good too strong. It's not good too weak. This is why I always strictly lecture our young guys on how to make tea, saying, "You idiot! It's not like if *agari* is bitter, then it's good!" You can only use the powders once. If you reuse them a second time, it doesn't taste good.

So if there are two customers, then we make exactly two servings of pow-

Place only as much tea powder as necessary in the strainer and pour hot water over it. Since the *agari* goes into a teapot first, it won't be scalding when it's served into a cup.

dered tea, then discard it. This way, we can always serve delicious tea.

Put tea powder corresponding to the number of people in a tea strainer, and then pour hot water for that number of people into a teapot. I get mad when the young guys make tea indifferently without a mind to such basic common sense.

Say you're serving *agari* to two customers. If an apprentice pours a lot of tea and there's still half a teapot left, what happens to it? You have to make hot tea all over again. This is how it gets to, "You idiot!"

If I'm just having some tea, I wouldn't holler even if it's too strong. But with *agari*, it's not like if it's bitter, it's good. Or if it's hot, it's good. The sourness of *kohada* (gizzard shad), the sweetness of the *nitsume* (reduction sauce) of *anago* (conger eel), the fat of *otoro* (fatty tuna), and the aroma of the ocean of *nori maki*—all of these need to be eliminated quickly with a sip or two of *agari*.

Some customers might like their *agari* bitter to the point that their faces twist. If a customer like that says, "Give me a bitter one," then you should make and serve a really strong tea.

First off, for *agari* and other matters, sushi restaurants have procedures that are common sense. "If you're aspiring to be a first-class pro, then follow that procedure."

That is what I want to say.

A sushi chef in the habit of using the same amount of powdered tea for when there are two customers, five customers, or eight customers will create waste elsewhere too. And when he becomes independent, he'll be in the red. But when it's completely ingrained in you while you're young that things belonging to other people are valuable, you're bound to treat your own things as valuable when you become independent.

It's not because I don't want to waste powdered tea or because my wealth decreases a little that I get angry. It's not that. It's that if they keep doing such things, they're never going to make it on their own. They'll never make delicious nigiri.

When I was in second grade, at the age of eight, I went to serve at a *kappo ryokan* (an inn serving high-end traditional cuisine) in Futamatacho (present-day Tenryu) in Shizuoka Prefecture, and I worked as an assistant in the kitchen while I went to school. Apart from my stint at a munitions plant and enlistment during the war, ever since second grade I've always held a kitchen knife and was taught to treat other people's things with care.

Even the young guys who work at our restaurant can't possibly stay as apprentice boys forever. Their fate is to start their own places in the future or to inherit their fathers' establishments. I want them to continue making nigiri in high spirits even when they're over seventy like me, so being strict with them is a part of my job.

I'll keep on scolding them for small mistakes if it has anything to do with sushi. No matter what they think of me, I'll stay the stubborn scary pops of a sushi restaurant.

I've started thinking things like that, too, lately.

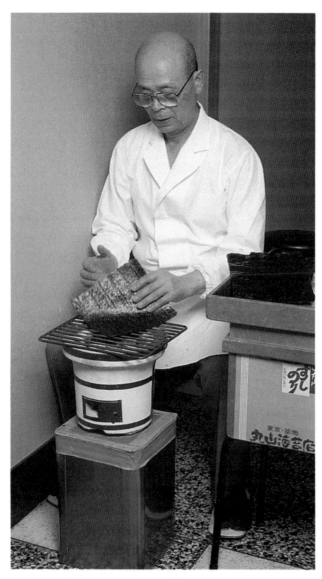

Jiro Ono roasts *nori*. Over blazing *bincho* charcoal,
heat at nearly a right angle and swiftly turn over—
a difficult technique.

Nori Maki, Tamagoyaki

Tekka Maki (tuna roll), (*chutoro*/medium-fatty tuna), May, Sado

Among Sukiyabashi Jiro orders, there are many for *chutoro*. Typically eaten dipped in *shoyu* (soy sauce) but served with *nikiri* brushed on it if a customer prefers.

Kyuri Maki (cucumber roll)

Two pieces of thin *murokyuri* (*muro* cucumber) as a core after removing the bumps, rolled with wasabi.

Oboro Maki (ground flesh roll)

The *ebi oboro* (ground flesh of shrimp) thin roll favored by regulars. Nice as a dessert of sorts to round out the meal.

Left: *nori* upon stocking
Right: grilled with *bincho* charcoal, turns vivid and aromatic

Anakyu Maki

The tail flesh from simmered *anago* (conger eel) and cucumber as the core, rolled with wasabi and brushed with *nitsume* (reduction sauce) on the surface.

Kanpyo Maki (dried gourd roll)

Back in the day, *nori maki* (roll wrapped in seaweed) meant thin *kanpyo maki*. The umami of *kanpyo* worked on for two days has depth. *Kanpyo maki* are usually cut into four pieces, the other thin rolls in six.

Sliced in two so it's easier to eat.

For orders of just the *tamagoyaki*, it's sliced into nigiri-*dane* size and brought to the counter.

Tamagoyaki (Japanese omelette)

Put a deep slit in *tamagoyaki* and make nigiri with it saddling. Less rice used than for other nigiri.

227

How to make *oboro*

Oboro Maki

Packed *barazushi*

Boil salt water, less salty than seawater, and put *kuruma ebi* in it.

Drain water in colander.

Ingredients: *mirin* (sweet rice wine), white granulated sugar, sea salt, *kuruma ebi* (prawn), and *shiba ebi* (shiba shrimp)

Once surface of *kuruma ebi* has slightly colored...

Divide boiled shrimp into three batches and put in food processor.

Remove *shiba ebi*'s heads, shells, and tails.

Add *shiba ebi*.

Add a little water so it'll be pasty, and switch on.

Peel shells off *kuruma ebi* as well. They can be leftover boiled ones.

Take out *shiba ebi* half-raw right before they are cooked through.

It turns into ground paste shortly.

Put *mirin* in the pot and heat it.

Once it starts to boil, lower heat and add ground *ebi*.

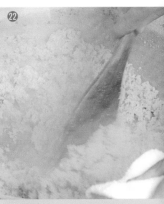

Keep roasting as long as it's steaming.

Add white granulated sugar, for a plainer sweetness than regular sugar.

Stir with wooden spoon to avoid clumping.

Forty minutes after roasting, take off of heat and dissipate residual warmth by stirring with wooden spoon.

Add pinch of sea salt.

Stir as if cutting with spoon so it doesn't burn or become sticky.

Done. Lasts about two weeks refrigerated.

Completely dissolve sugar.

Keep at it.

How to cook *kanpyo*
(dried gourd)

Cut 400 g of dried *kanpyo* to the width of *nori* (dried seaweed).

Soak in water and restore.

Softens overnight.

Discard water and sprinkle two pinches of salt.

Massage with both hands until soft.

Rinse with water. Keep changing water to remove salt.

Put *kanpyo* in large pot, fill with water, and heat over high flame.

Stir once in a while to avoid tangling.

Check *kanpyo* while it's boiling. It's good when you can insert your nail.

Remove from heat and cool with water.

Squeeze lightly with both hands, trying not to squash *kanpyo*.

Drain in colander.

230

Spread *kanpyo*, remove hard parts, and trim edges.

Now uniform in thickness, length, and width.

Put water and granulated white sugar in pot and bring to boil.

Add *shoyu* (soy sauce) when sugar has melted.

Bring back to a boil.

Unravel *kanpyo* and place in pot.

Spread and stew in just enough fluid to cover.

Once broth boils, flip *kanpyo* upside down.

Try to avoid uneven cooking.

Grab pot with both hands to toss *kanpyo*, instead of using *saibashi* (long chopsticks).

Simmer until all of the broth has soaked into *kanpyo*.

Once done, place in a colander to cool so it doesn't get soggy.

231

How to roll
(thin roll)
hoso maki
(*Kanpyo*/dried gourd)

Leave about 5 mm on your side on *nori*.

Place *kanpyo* in the middle of sushi rice.

Place one roll worth of sushi rice on *nori* on top of *makisu* with the front side of *nori* facing down.

Press down *kanpyo* with middle fingers, lift up your side of *makisu* with thumbs, and roll in one go.

Press down while trying not to squash grains and spread sushi rice.

Tighten *makisu* without having it catch.

Push both edges to keep contents from spilling.

Spread it evenly into the edges.

With where the *nori* meets on bottom, adjust shape into square.

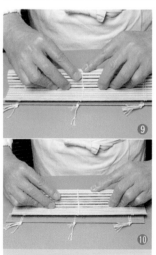
Spread it toward you.

Rolling done. *Kanpyo maki* is cut into four. Slice roll in half and then in half again.

232

Chapter 5

Of

Sumeshi

Barazushi **(for six people)** Only if there's time. It's sushi for takeout.

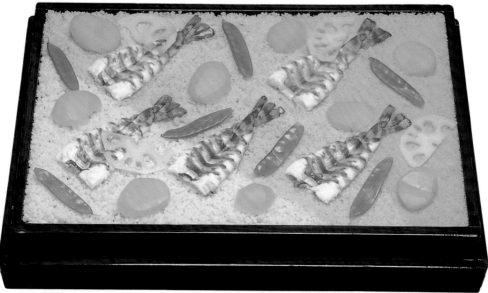

Sanshoku (tricolor) *chirashi*

A *barazushi* variation, special-order *chirashi-zushi*. Tricolor: egg yolk *oboro*, whitefish *oboro*, and *ebi* (shrimp) *oboro*.

Chirashi-zushi

Not normally made, but some deliveries in the immediate neighborhood. From front: *aji*/horse mackerel (Futtsu), *kuruma ebi*/prawn (Tokyo Bay), *aka gai*/surf clam (Yuriage), *mako garei*/marbled sole (Joban), *aori ika*/bigfin reef squid (Nagasaki), *kinusaya*/snow pea, candied chestnut, *kohada*/gizzard shad (Kyushu), *chutoro*/medium-fatty tuna (Sado), *shiitake*, *subasu*/vinegared lotus root, *tamagoyaki*/Japanese omelette, *hamabofu*/beach silvertop, *anago*/conger eel (Nojima); diced *kanpyo* (dried gourd) and *shoga* (ginger) on top of *sumeshi* (vinegared rice), and crumbled *nori* (dried seaweed).

Chirashi-zushi

(variety of toppings, mainly seafood, on top of a bed of rice)

Three Kinds

235

How to make *barazushi*

Put sushi rice in tray.

Spread evenly.

Dice *kanpyo* and *shoga* and sprinkle them on top.

Sprinkle crumbled *nori*.

Slice stewed *shiitake* into thin strips and sprinkle evenly.

Sprinkle thinly sliced *kohada*.

The simmered *anago* should be chopped coarsely.

Diced for the *tamagoyaki*.

Spread toppings evenly so the guests could start anywhere.

9

Decorate with *kuruma ebi*.

13

Arrange thin slices of *subasu* in radial pattern.

10

Add *kinusaya* for color.

14

Pack *oboro* from edge of tray.

11

Finished. *Tane* changes by season, but never raw items.

15

Thinly pack all over on the surface. Adjust the sweetness with amount of *oboro*.

12

In the case of *oribako* (folding box)

Moisten bamboo leaves and pack on bottom and edges of box.

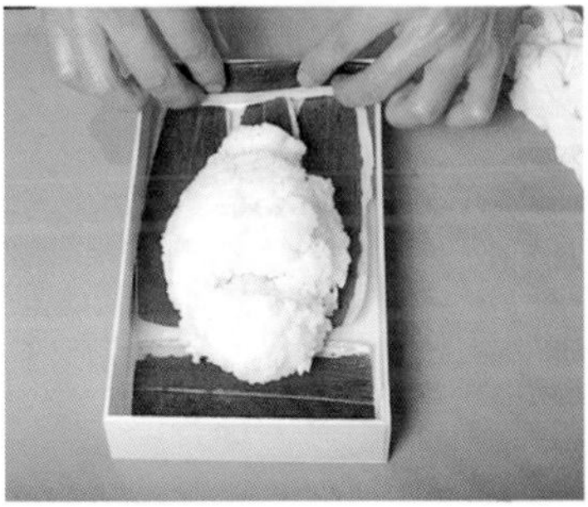

237

How to make sushi rice

Put 10 cups of rice in a 20-cup *hagama* (old-fashioned rice cooker).

Rinse rice and pour out water (filtered, purified). Repeat twice. When you rinse it too much, the rice grains crack, so be careful.

Pour water and rinse, three times until water isn't cloudy.

Decide on amount of filtered, purified water using your hand as a measure and taking the quality of rice into consideration.

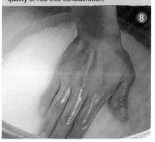

Put iron lid on rice cooker.

Add more weight by placing a wooden lid and a container filled with water on top.

Start on high heat, and once you see steam, lower to medium heat.

Heat over medium heat for ten minutes, over low for ten minutes, and lastly over high heat for five seconds, then turn off heat. Let steam for fifteen minutes.

238

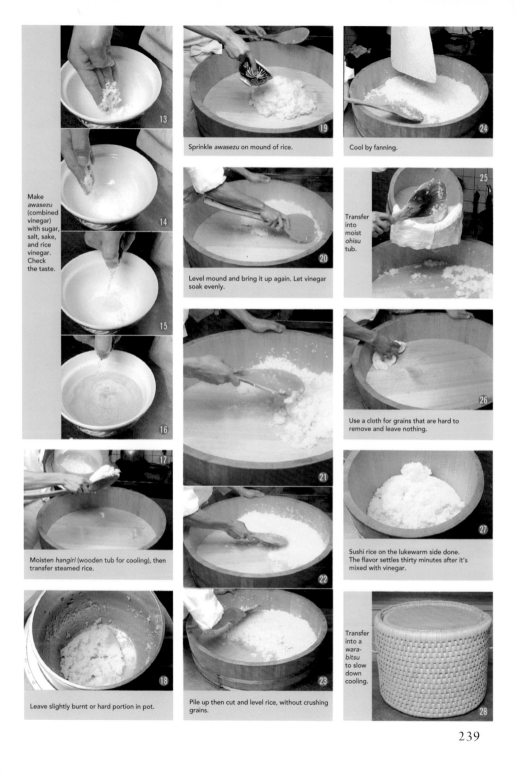

Make *awasezu* (combined vinegar) with sugar, salt, sake, and rice vinegar. Check the taste.

Sprinkle *awasezu* on mound of rice.

Cool by fanning.

Level mound and bring it up again. Let vinegar soak evenly.

Transfer into moist *ohisu* tub.

Moisten *hangiri* (wooden tub for cooling), then transfer steamed rice.

Use a cloth for grains that are hard to remove and leave nothing.

Leave slightly burnt or hard portion in pot.

Sushi rice on the lukewarm side done. The flavor settles thirty minutes after it's mixed with vinegar.

Pile up then cut and level rice, without crushing grains.

Transfer into a *wara-bitsu* to slow down cooling.

239

How to make nigiri

(Jiro Ono is left-handed)

Dip left fingertips into *tezu*, diluted vinegar with water.

Transfer *tezu* to right hand and moisten.

Take sushi rice with left hand.

Pick up *tane* with right hand and hold firmly with thumb.

Pick up wasabi with left index finger...

...and place in middle of *tane*.

Place sushi rice on *tane*.

With right thumb, press down lightly on rice.

Cover sushi rice with left index and middle fingers and clasp.

Stretch right fingers and use momentum to turn nigiri halfway around with *tane* on top.

Pinch and press both sides of nigiri with left fingers.

Bend right fingers, take nigiri, and press down *tane* with two left fingers.

With left hand, rotate nigiri halfway counter-clockwise.

Put nigiri on the base of right fingers.

Press down on tane with right thumb and hold both sides of nigiri with left thumb and inside fingers.

Bend right fingers lightly and prepare for next step.

Hold down tane with left index and middle fingers and edge of nigiri with right thumb.

Second round. Rotate nigiri halfway counter-clockwise and hold down on sides of nigiri and on top of tane.

Rotate nigiri halfway counter-clockwise for third time and as before hold down and tighten on sides of nigiri and on top of tane.

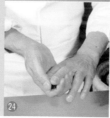

Rotate nigiri halfway counterclockwise for fourth time.

Tighten both sides of nigiri.

Using two left fingers, tighten top of tane, and further tighten by pulling tane toward you, and the nigiri is done.

Hold both sides to serve.

241

How to pickle *shoga*
(ginger)

After chilling hands in water, squeeze hot ginger, carefully so as not to tear the thin slices.

Peel skin off of young ginger and shave thin.

Temper spiciness by pouring hot water on young ginger. If it's not young, then only run through hot water.

Young ginger reddens gradually.

It's still vinegarish now. Good to eat after half a day.

How to grate wasabi

Shave dirt off 3-year-old wasabi from Amagi, and grate in spirals from head so it's sticky. A little at a time, and use from a small plate.

Marinate ginger in sweet vinegar (mix white granulated sugar, vinegar, and salt, bring to boil, and chill). Once pickled, it starts to turn reddish.

242

JIRO SUSHI TALK 5

OF *SUMESHI*

"You absolutely cannot make delicious sushi if the vinegared rice isn't at body temperature."

The nigiri that Jiro Ono makes is beautiful whenever I look at it. And his handsome nigiri, which doesn't collapse even when I pick it up with chopsticks, softly falls apart once it's in my mouth, blending together with the *tane* and slipping down my throat. What they say—"the flavor of nigiri is four parts *tane* and six parts rice"—is the ultimate truth. That's why the last "Sushi Talk" concerns *sumeshi* (vinegared rice).

The most important thing for nigiri is *sumeshi* (vinegared rice) when all is said and done. You can't make good nigiri on a foundation of badly made *shari* (argot for "vinegared rice"), no matter what supreme *neta* you've lined up. It's not as if you can only use such-and-such a brand of rice, but the grains should be as small as possible, and yet oily and firm.

Shari should be cooked on the firm side. If it doesn't contain oil, then it becomes dry, but if you increase the water it's cooked in, it becomes too

243

sticky. To have a fluffy finish, it has to contain oil, generally speaking.

When I ask the rice dealer, a pro among pros, he says the most appropriate kind for *sumeshi* is small-grain rice from mountain valleys where there is a drastic range in temperature—sunny from morning to evening, and chilly come evening.

Plains that are suitable for mass cultivation tend not to see that fluctuation. For instance, the *koshihikari* new rice harvested on the flatlands in Niigata Prefecture surely tastes great while it's still hot, right after being cooked, precisely because it's soft, but it doesn't make for good *sumeshi*. *Shari* has to retain a complete delicious flavor even after the rice cools down to body temperature. In that respect, the pro says that the taste of the oily small-grain rice is the most consistent.

This is why I mainly use rice harvested in the mountain valleys of Toyama Prefecture that was recommended to me. And if you cook such *etchumai* well, then even after mixing in the vinegar, it doesn't get sticky, and it falls apart softly in the mouth. We talk about "*shari* standing up," and when each grain stands on its own, the *sumeshi* melts and becomes integrated with the *neta* the moment they go into your mouth. It would be troubling if it stayed bunched up in a ball in your mouth forever.

We make rice with an iron *hagama* (old-fashioned rice cooker) and keep it warm by storing it in a *warabitsu* (straw tub)

We cook *shari* (vinegared rice) three times during our three and a half evening hours.

Typically sushi restaurants make an amount called *ippon*. That equals two *sho* (3 kilograms), but we only make one *sho* (1.5 kilograms). Putting aside places with very high turnover rates, if you store two *sho* of rice in the basin, the bottom part gets hard by getting pressed down, so there is no way you can make delicious nigiri. I think so, so it's one *sho*.

We cook rice rinsed with filtered water under high pressure without letting any steam escape. We use an iron *hagama* with a thick iron lid, and a massive amount of water goes on top as weight. The power of steam isn't to be underestimated. The pressure is tremendous. I mean, it even allows heavy locomotive trains to run choo-choo. (See photo on page 238.)

This is why, when the pressure increases in the rice cooker, the iron lid with a weight on it lifts up. If it's a wooden lid, by contrast, the steam escapes somehow and the lid doesn't rise. If you don't use that much pressure, it doesn't come out fluffy.

Watching the steam spout, you make small adjustments by lowering the flame and shifting the lid. In the end, human handling makes a difference. It doesn't go that way with a pressure cooker.

So, well, I believe that's the secret to making ideal *shari,* and I keep at it.

Of course, for heating power, firewood is the best. However, I can't use any in the basement of a building in the middle of Tokyo, so I cook with high-calorie gas. In this day and age you even bake porcelain with electricity or gas rather than in a climbing kiln.

Right before the rice is done cooking, to get rid of the excess moisture, we turn up the heat once. Then it inevitably gets burned. After removing the *kamasoko okoge* (burned rice at the cooker's bottom), you get about seven or eight *go* (1 to 1.2 kg) that become *shari*. If we cook more, we can't keep it at body temperature, neither warm nor cool to the touch.

Many customers are attuned to the *neta's* flavor, but few pay attention to the temperature gap with *shari*. If the *shari* isn't at body temperature, the nigiri's taste will never be consistent. If it's hot or cold, it changes drastically. I believe in this, so I keep at it. *Shari* that has cooled and balled really doesn't taste good and is so difficult to make nigiri with that you swear, "I'm never doing this again."

When the *shari* is tight, you're tempted to throw in an extra *tekaeshi* (technique for turning nigiri) because you can't make it as you want with the usual count. But you mustn't. The tighter the *shari*, the softer the nigiri needs to be. It would be much easier to do another *tekaeshi*, since that way, the *shari* profile assumes the paper-fan shape basic to the *Edomae* style.

There is subtlety in the way nigiri is made, and I assume that makes the difference: "That chef's nigiri tastes delicious," "That chef's doesn't."

At the same time, if you hurriedly make nigiri while the rice is still hot because you feel bad about making them wait, it doesn't come out so well either. The *shari* sticks to your hands. Of course it does. The vinegar hasn't soaked through yet. The outside is sticky, and the inside is still hard. It can't possibly taste good.

But after half an hour, it absorbs the vinegar, the firmness of each grain has come to be suitable, and your touch can be gentle. In other words, it's *shari* at body temperature that I can make nigiri with comfortably, and that's the most delicious moment to have it.

To keep *shari* at body temperature, we store it in *warabitsu*. Every household owned *warabitsu* back in the day, but let alone making them, very few people even know what it is. What we use now was made to order in a village up in the mountains on the Yamagata-Niigata prefectural border. We don't use a rice cooker to force the rice to stay warm using electricity, but instead surround the wooden basin with *warabitsu*. This merely slows down the rate the rice cools at. While I'm making nigiri, the wooden basin is wide open, you see.

But it's best to apply this natural way for *shari*. If not, we can't make delicious nigiri. I'm certain of it, so in preparation for "*warabitsu* extinction day," which may arrive soon, I have a few replacements.

I'm often told that my customers don't get thirsty after eating our nigiri

Bumper rice crops have continued lately—it's the worst for sushi chefs. Rice plants showered with sunlight grow too much, and the grains start to split. When we cook rice like that, the starch flows out and no matter how we make nigiri with it, it clumps.

It's especially bad in the new rice season. From October to the following March, when we get new rice, we mix old rice that contains less moisture in with the new so it doesn't stick. Normally, this makes it good. But if the previous year had a bumper crop, even the old rice is very starchy. It doesn't make a difference even if I mix some in.

This is from long experience. I touch rice all the time over the course of the year. "Ack, no good"—I can tell as soon as I put my hands in the wooden basin. Maybe I can trick the customers' tongues with how I make the nigiri, but I can't trick my own hands. I end up hastily cooking the next batch.

My way of making nigiri is to tighten just the outside and to leave the inside loose, but if the rice is too starchy, I can't pull off that trick. If I make it gently, then the shape collapses, but if I apply too much force, it gets packed to the core. In bad cases, out of seven or eight *go* (1 to 1.2 kg), it stays fine until about the third *go*, but after the fourth they start to bunch up into dumplings.

Especially during the afternoon, there aren't many people who drink sake, so I just go on making nigiri. On average, one customer has about fourteen to fifteen pieces. Three to four *go* (450 to 600 g) of rice quickly disappear after I serve fifty to sixty pieces. It takes about an hour to cook *shari* and cool it down to body temperature, so if it's busy like that, even if we make one batch after another, we're behind.

No, it's not that we run out. There it is, right in front of the guests. I have no choice but to make dumpling nigiri with it until the next batch arrives.

If a customer tilts his head and wonders out loud, "Weird. Not like usual," then I explain, "Yes, you noticed. The rice lately is so starchy that it starts to bunch up into dumplings." But for the customer, it's not his problem.

"Whether the rice is good or bad, the sushi restaurant master's job is to come up with a way to make delicious sushi."

He doesn't say this out loud, but that's probably what he's thinking. Because it's not like we give discounts when the rice is in bad condition. We charge the same price as always.

So I was very close to having a nervous breakdown, and I made an unreasonable demand to the rice pro to run around and search for a product that doesn't bunch up into dumplings.

In the end, the kind I use now is similar because it's also from a bumper crop, but when I cook it, it comes out so much better. When I asked the rice dealer, he told me that the starch content is the same, but the one I was using before was electrically dried, while the current one is sun-dried. The farmers had set it aside for their own delectation. That's how much more delicious sun-dried rice is.

It goes to show how excellent the rice that the old ladies carried from Ryugasaki (Ibaraki Prefecture) in the past was, and I mean up until about 1987. Forget all the logic. Their rice was sincerely delicious. No matter how poorly the crop turned out during the year, there were no extreme differences in flavor like there are now.

Customers often tell me that they don't get thirsty after eating our nigiri. I used to explain, "You don't because we've always used unrefined salt containing bittern from salt pans, not refined salt that's just salty. It's probably thanks to the quality of salt." Of course, it could be attributed to our use of unrefined salt, but our *shari* is, after all, lighted seasoned.

According to Kyobashi's master chef, *shari* back in the day had more vinegar in it. Only salt and vinegar were mixed in, and they didn't use sugar.

That's because vinegar was stored in wooden barrels back then. When it rested for a year, one *to* (18 liters) decreased to about eight *sho* (14.4 liters), and as the content thickened, the sweetness came out, and it started to get a little red. When you added a little bit of salt, the sweetness actually increased. It's the same as putting salt on a summer tangerine; the tanginess goes away.

However, vinegar like that disappeared from the world. Maybe because the containers changed, the vinegar I use now doesn't dissipate at all after sitting for a year, though the flavor itself isn't bad. This is why we add very little sugar, to the point where the customers don't even notice. It gives a shine to the vinegared rice and also takes the edge off the sourness and saltiness, creating a rounded flavor.

We only add a little bit of sugar because if you make it sweeter, the customers won't be able to enjoy as many pieces.

When you're starving, the first few nigiri feel more delicious when they're on the sweet rather than sour side. But that's it. After ten pieces or so, you don't want more.

But if it has a lighter flavor, then you can have fifteen or sixteen pieces, and even twenty if you're really hungry. My thinking is that nigiri should be lightly flavored enough so that after you leave our restaurant, you feel, "Ahhh, I could've had more."

It's after the war that nigiri got smaller

Here's what I think regarding the size of nigiri. To sum up, there is a suitable size when you put it in your mouth: it tastes the best when you can eat it in one bite. And it's not nigiri if you can't taste the *shari*, so it shouldn't be any smaller.

I never measured it, but out of one *go* (150 g) of rice, I make about sixteen or seventeen pieces of nigiri. I've always made it that size, ever since I became the master of a sushi restaurant.

Meanwhile, from the Meiji period to early Showa (1868-1930s), "a-bite-and-a-half pieces" were the norm. Apparently they were so big that you couldn't have it in one bite. It was three times bigger than my nigiri, so you probably had five to six pieces at most. It was only after the war that the size got smaller.

Lately, the standard for one person for delivery or an assorted plate seems to be "ten pieces, counting the rolls," but there was a reason for it.

After the war, food was extremely scarce. It wasn't even a question of making nigiri; using rice from the black market could get you arrested. So some clever guy at one of the sushi restaurants thought of something. How about if customers brought their rationed rice and had the chefs make nigiri in exchange for that rice? The restaurants could charge for the *neta* and processing. In other words, "processing on consignment" of nigiri *zushi*. That way, you didn't break the laws prohibiting sales of rice.

Based on that understanding back around in 1947, they decided to make ten pieces of nigiri including *makimono* (rolled items) for each *go*. This was for one person, so each piece of nigiri got much smaller.

By the way, when I began my apprenticeship at Kyobashi Restaurant, all sorts of small colorful bags were piled up in the corner. It was six years after we lost the war, and by then we could make nigiri without people bringing their own rice. But when the police came to check, we needed to show proof of "processing on consignment." The bags were there to pretend that the rice had been brought by our customers. If they were all the same bags, the authorities would catch on to us, so we had bags in all sorts of colors and materials like cotton and paper.

The balance between *neta* and *shari* has remained the same ever since. There are sushi restaurants that serve extremely large *neta* or extremely small *shari*. However, if the *neta* is too big or the *shari* too small, the top overwhelms the flavor and you can't discern the deliciousness of *shari*. It's no longer nigiri. So I believe my way is the best.

But if I'm serving a senior citizen, I make the *shari* smaller. I look at my guests and change how I make nigiri. If it's an assorted plate, then I make larger pieces so a customer can get full from an order for one, and I make them firmer since the customer will be using chopsticks. If I don't, by the time he touches it, the *shari* might split. Because he's going, "Should I eat this one or that one."

And for guests from foreign countries, I make the nigiri super firm and tight. Since those folks dip the *shari*, not the *neta*, in the *shoyu* (soy sauce), I make nigiri that doesn't fall apart even when they dunk it in. So firm that a Japanese customer would say, "You expect me to eat this?"

Another thing. For a party of two customers, I want them to eat the same amount, so for the woman, I make smaller nigiri. Only to such a slight degree that the average person can't tell. Keep on using smaller amounts, and the difference comes out to a whole piece or two.

"I had as much as my husband." The ladies love that.

Over seventy and so much more to learn

By the way, what determines the flavor of nigiri is not just the *shari* and *neta*. The wasabi, *nikiri* (thin and sweet glaze), and *nitsume* (reduction sauce) that act as go-betweens are also important. Wasabi is an especially outstanding supporting actor. What I use is three years old, from Amagi in Izu. The color, aroma, spiciness, and sweetness of *honwasabi* from Amagi are consistently wonderful.

Even so, it's challenging to determine the amount of wasabi to use. If it sticks out too much, the *neta*'s flavor is eliminated, but if you don't taste it, then the nigiri feels out of tune.

"Such a delicious nigiri, I can sense the aroma of wasabi," is the appropriate amount.

Interestingly, depending on the *neta*, the wasabi feels stronger or weaker. For rich *otoro* (fatty tuna) and *uni* (sea urchin), you can't taste it unless I use a good dollop. On the other hand, for plain *kohada* (gizzard shad), *ika* (squid), and white and red meat, if I apply just a third of the amount for *otoro*, it feels plenty spicy.

Especially with *ika*, putting too much wasabi is a no-no. If you put on too much, it stings the nose, the tears flow, and you don't even know if it tasted good when it goes down your throat. It's not like wasabi is doing its job as long as it stings.

We serve raw seafood, silver-skinned fish, and *awabi* (abalone) with *nikiri*, and *anago* (conger eel) and *hamaguri* (hard clam) with *nitsume* brushed on them. *Nikiri* is a reduction of seven parts *shoyu* (soy sauce) and three parts sake, roughly speaking. Three parts and seven make ten. But boil it down to seven. That way, because sake is in the mix, the flavor changes a little bit. I don't like an overly rich taste, so I only use a little bit of *mirin* (sweet rice wine) as a hidden flavor. Of course, I don't use MSG, either. I also make our *nitsume* so that it comes out light and plain to go well with our *anago* and *hamaguri*. As for brands of *shoyu*, I use the ones from Gobo (Wakayama Prefecture), or Karuizawa, or Kanazawa Prefecture. If a good one comes out, I go for it. Right now we use the one from Kanazawa. For *shoyu*, it's not like "the more expensive, the better." There are companies that put on expensive price tags and shamelessly use refined salt.

We offer a small *shoyu* plate even when the nigiri is brushed with *nikiri* so that you can dip the ungarnished *tekka maki* (tuna roll) or *kyuri maki* (cucumber roll) in the *shoyu* yourself. If a customer feels that the amount of *nikiri* that I put on isn't enough, I don't mind if a nigiri gets dipped, too.

However, there are customers who dunk pieces that I want them to eat as is, like *kanpyo maki* (dried gourd roll), *tamagoyaki* (Japanese omelette), and *anago* and *hamaguri*, which have *nitsume* on them. I used to get mad whenever I saw them do that, but now that I'm over seventy, I try not to mind. It's not good for my heart.

By the way, the other day someone asked me, "Your vinegared rice goes well with any *tane*, whether it's whitefish, silver-skinned fish, or *anago*, even *tamagoyaki* and *makimono* (rolled items), but why is that?"

Our *shari* goes well with *kohada* (gizzard shad). And *nori maki* (dried gourd roll). I've always thought so. But to be honest, I never audaciously planned for our *shari* to accommodate the flavor of all the *neta*.

I gave some thought as to why I'd been told that.

Every place has its own quirks for sushi rice—say, the vinegar might be strong or it might be on the salty side—but maybe our *shari* has a much lighter flavor that even I knew. I came to realize this. It's because the taste is much lighter than I thought that it goes well with any *neta*. Maybe that's what that customer was saying.

If either the vinegar or salt is strong, then it goes well with sweet *anago*, but not with sour *kohada*. Balances like that will come into play. But neither the salt nor the vinegar sticks out in our *shari*. It has a rather rounded flavor, and the sweetness also doesn't stand out like with *sumeshi* from the Kyoto and Osaka area.

So I thought about it long and hard again.

He'd said that it went well with both *kohada* and *anago*, but when each *neta* has a different flavor, and provided the condition and temperature of *shari* is the same, shouldn't there actually be some marginal issues in the taste? Because the flavors of *neta* on top are all different—the pickled one, the sweetened one, some with just the fish's inherent flavor. I just can't get my head around the logic of it.

I'm over seventy but have so much more to learn.

IDLE TALK BETWEEN A SUSHI RESTAURANT POPS AND HIS REGULAR

Jiro Ono
Shinzo Satomi

It's already been twenty years since I (Satomi) started going to Sukiyabashi Jiro. That's because the rhythm of Jiro Ono making his nigiri is as comfortable as "man and horse become one." Unless you order lots of expensive *tane*, the bill won't make you turn blue, either. With the publication of this book as my unique tender, and exercising my special privileges as a regular, I inquired after the sushi restaurant pops' true feelings. And what would you know...

The reason *ichinin-mae* (an order for one) is a special bargain

Satomi: From the very start, this may feel like Zen questions and answers, but what is the attraction of *Edomae*-style nigiri?

Ono: As long as you don't cause trouble for people around you, eat what you like. Eat however many you want. Eat it with your hands or with chopsticks. I think that's the biggest attraction of *Edomae*-style nigiri. Because the stocking price is high lately, there is a sense of, you know, luxury to nigiri *zushi*. The sushi craftsmen make nigiri with that in mind, and the customers also think it's natural for nigiri *zushi* to be expensive. But nigiri was originally for the people. It began with food stands.

Satomi: Because top-class restaurants don't display their prices, the customers never know how much they'll get charged. So they chicken out. What do you think about that from an owner-chef perspective?

Ono: Many people may feel at a loss for the first time. But in the end, it's all about how you eat. In the beginning, order *ichinin-mae* (an order for one). For instance, we have two kinds, at either 4,000 yen or 5,000 yen. When you're done, you have a rough sense of the flavor and price of Sukiyabashi Jiro. Try prix-fixe

The 5000-yen *ichinin-mae* assortment served at the tables. Eight *kan* of nigiri and one *hosomaki*: on this day, *aori ika, kuruma ebi, kohada, anago, chutoro, mako garei, maguro* (lean meat), *kyuri maki,* and *tamagoyaki*. The items depend on the day, but it's a bargain—20% cheaper than ordering à la carte.

ichinin-mae, and if you're absolutely convinced, then make a reservation to sit at the counter and eat à la carte.

Satomi: If the ten pieces in *ichinin-mae* cost 4,000 yen then the average piece is 400 yen. But when it comes to eating à la carte, it gets more expensive. And I think people simply wonder why.

Ono: *Ichinin-mae* is a bargain that we serve to customers at our table seats. And the master of the sushi restaurant decides the featured *neta*. However, when a customer orders, "Make nigiri with *mushi awabi* (steamed abalone)," then we absolutely have to accommodate the order no matter what, even if I know a regular who likes *awabi* is coming later. There is no need to use such a *neta* for *ichinin-mae*.

Satomi: Yes, of course.

Ono: As a sushi restaurant pops, I have to say, people who blindly go, "I like *uni* (sea urchin), I like *aka gai* (surf clam), I like *otoro* (fatty tuna)," and then, "Can I get the bill?" and gets angry—"Why is it so expensive!"—when I answer "Yes, 35,000 yen please," really don't know nigiri *neta* and their prices. It may sound like I'm trying to bamboozle you or something, but if you want to eat at a sushi restaurant

255

of a certain level, then it's better to equip yourself with a fair amount of preliminary knowledge.

Satomi: I always tell young guys, "You're ten years too young to eat *A, I, U, E, O*": *awabi* (abalone), *aka gai* (surf clam), *ikura* (salmon roe), *uni* (sea urchin), *ebi* (shrimp), and *otoro* (fatty tuna)." *Odori* (raw prawn), which you don't carry, isn't cheap either. They should order *tane* like that when they get older. I have no idea if they are trust-fund babies or not, but there is nothing more unpleasant than seeing young guys wolf down *A, I, U, E, O* like they own the place.

Ono: Ha ha ha.

Satomi: In the evening, do many customers drink sake, picking at whitefish, before moving on to nigiri?

Ono: Yes, that's most of them.

Satomi: The experts say, "There's nothing better than green tea for *Edomae*-style nigiri," but I guess that's not the case at *Jiro*.

Ono: Correct. It may be fine for people who don't like to drink, but for people who like to drink, dinner means their minds switch to "night" mode. Then they feel like starting with a drink before getting into the nigiri.

Satomi: Sushi restaurants serve the best-quality fish in Tokyo. Regular traditional restaurants only serve *tai* (sea bream), *meji* (young tuna), *ika* (squid), and shellfish.

Ono: That's absolutely right.

For some reason, I forget to charge for *otoro* (fatty tuna)

Satomi: By the way, how do sushi chefs calculate the bill while entertaining multiple customers?

Ono: Of course, it's all by memory. I don't calculate on the spot if it's *okuri* (billing later). I look at the stocking receipt later when I'm keeping books and say, "I made nigiri with it, I didn't make nigiri with it, I didn't make nigiri with it, I made nigiri with it." So it's a huge trouble on days when there are many customers who pay with cash. I have to memorize everything for two, three, four parties.

Satomi: I heard stories of chefs using rice grains as an abacus.

Ono: Yeah, with that, you'd see if you tried it yourself, but it's so much more efficient to memorize than to take and arrange rice grains one by one out of the rice bowl. I can't be bothered with such a troublesome task when I'm busy.

Satomi: Ha ha ha. I see. I can see that.

Ono: The reason I don't grow senile is because I'm using my head twenty-four-seven. That's what my regulars say.

Satomi: If I may be so bold as to ask, are your calculations accurate?

Ono: Of course they're accurate. I swear by heaven and earth that I've never once miscalculated and overcharged a customer. That's never happened even once, but sometimes I charge less than I should. Carelessly, by mistake.

Satomi: Oh, why is that?

Ono: I forget what I made nigiri with. What's more, if it's *kohada* (gizzard shad) or *iwashi* (sardine) that's fairly reasonable to stock, then fine, but I tend to forget to charge for the expensive *neta* like *uni* (sea urchin) and *aka gai* (surf clam).

Satomi: I see.

Ono: Which *neta* do you think is easiest for me to forget?

Satomi: Tell me.

Ono: It's *otoro*.

Satomi: What? That's a huge amount of money since one piece of *otoro* costs the same as five pieces of *kohada*. If a hypnotist became your regular, you'd be in deep trouble. But customers at *Jiro* must always eat *kohada* and *anago* (conger eel), while *otoro* can't be one of the *tane* that they always order.

Ono: The guests have *chutoro* (medium-fatty tuna). Say for ten *chutoro*, it's four to five lean meat, and three *otoro*.

Satomi: I wonder why you forget *otoro*. If you only occasionally make nigiri with it, then you should remember. *Otoro* is expensive, so there are many customers who balk at ordering it. Maybe you forget thanks to their accumulated grudge.

Ono: Ha ha ha. It's actually a simple story. Other *neta* only have one kind. But with *maguro* (tuna) there are three kinds—*otoro*, *chutoro*, and lean meat. And most of the guests have *chutoro*, then move onto something else, then lean meat, then *otoro*. After the meal, I clearly remember the *chutoro* and lean meat, but mysteriously, I completely forget about the *otoro* that I served last. So, yeah, it's a strange logic, but anyway, I forget the *otoro*. But I'm pretty sure I'm not the only one who does.

Satomi: A sushi master with a pessimistic personality must be doom and gloom all day.

Ono: Of course, when I charge, I'm certain there is no mistake. And alas, it tends to be after the restaurant closes that I realize, "What? For the customers who paid with cash, I forgot to charge for two pieces of *otoro*." If I noticed on the spot, I'd chase after them to get the money.

Satomi: If you were a master for hire, then it'd be a big problem. You couldn't tell your sponsor even if they tore your mouth open.

257

Ono: There was a period when I feigned innocence.

Satomi: Jiro, it's been thirty-plus years since you became a master chef. If we added up the amount of *otoro* you forgot...

Ono: It would be a great amount of money. I think it would be massive.

Satomi: One million yen wouldn't cover it.

Ono: Not at all. The most disastrous case was when four customers came for the first time. I completely forgot that I'd served four pieces of *otoro* per person at the beginning of their meal. That was big. It was four people. At 10,000 yen per person, it comes out to 40,000 yen. I think it was about 6,000 to 7,000 yen back then since other *neta* were fairly reasonable as well. Let's say it cost 6,000 yen, then it's 24,000 yen. Since I gave them such a huge discount, I expected them to visit often, saying, "Such a well-meaning restaurant is rare these days," but that quartet never showed up again.

Satomi: Maybe they felt guilty.

Ono: They knew I'd forgotten to charge them.

Satomi: Maybe they started running right after they left, saying, "That went well."

Ono: It's been ten years since then, but I remember their faces. I hope it was my last time forgetting to charge for a group order of *otoro* appetizers.

Satomi: So when customers pay with cash, you can memorize all the items they had?

Ono: If I don't, it gets all messed up halfway through, and in the end I won't know what to charge.

Satomi: It's like pro *shogi* (Japanese chess) players smoothly noting their every move after the game.

Ono: Yes. It's a benefit of training.

Who are his "welcome guests" and "unwelcome guests"

Satomi: Two pairs of customers, one with a pretty lady and one not, ate the same *tane* in the same order, but their bills weren't the same. I saw this experiment on TV. Does something like this happen in reality?

Ono: Yes, it does. What I mean to say, despite the possibility of being misunderstood, is that even for those of us in the business of serving customers, there are ones who're welcome to visit again and others whom I don't want to see again. A customer who horses around as much as he wants, and then lectures about how there is no one greater than he is, and who overstays his welcome, gets a higher bill for his behavior. If he complains, "Why is it so expensive?" then I talk back and say, "You occupied the seat for such a long time, this is reasonable." That's the only resistance the master of a sushi restaurant can put up.

Satomi: Customers pay money and you serve them. There's a strange trend to blur the line between chef and guest, but especially at sushi restaurants that are regarded as high-class, some customers address the master chefs so arrogantly.

Ono: Let's say there are two customers who are taking the same amount of time drinking. But there is a clear difference between them, so I feel, "Oh no, I don't want this customer ever to come back again," while "This person makes me feel pleasant"—all by how they drink, how they speak, and how they eat. If the two pairs of customers on TV really ate in the same order, with the same rhythm, at the same speed, and left saying, "Thanks for the meal," then I'm sure the bills would have come out the same. If not, then I think it's natural for there to be a big gap in the price.

Satomi: It's an extremely provocative statement, but I'm sure every sushi restaurant pops feels that way deep down. But they can't express how they really feel because they are in the vulnerable customer-service business.

Ono: Some actress on TV was really upset, saying, "I only ate eight pieces, but such and such a place charged me 80,000 yen." I wondered, "How many hours did she stay there?" If you only focus on the food, then 10,000 yen per nigiri seems outrageous, but if she was blabbing on for three hours at that restaurant, then 80,000 yen is rather cheap. In three hours, a busy sushi restaurant can turn over customers a couple of times. She snatched those profits. However, the part about "80,000 yen for eight pieces of nigiri" keeps getting embellished. She's not capable of thinking, "I stayed there from this hour to that hour and inconvenienced them." As soon as she mentioned how expensive it was, the show's sensible host or someone else there should have questioned her.

Satomi: I see.

Ono: Also, customers like that not only cause trouble for the restaurant by staying too long, but also for the other guests. They start to talk to strangers or pour sake, saying, "Here, how about a glass." If their neighbors wanted to drink sake, they'd order it themselves and have as much as they wanted. I don't like people like that. I really don't like insensitive people who start to chat with people they don't know. So, hoping that they'll never come back, I charge a high price. I'd be troubled if they still came. If they came often saying, "I don't really care if it's expensive," I'd be in real trouble.

Satomi: People like that are insensitive, so I'm sure they'll come back again.

Ono: Maybe.

Satomi: By the way, if we're not careful, I'm afraid readers will misunderstand your statement, so by way of caution I ask you, that kind of insensitive customer...

Ono: ...comes once in ten years.

Satomi: I feel better hearing that. So it's not like Sukiyabashi Jiro is a scary restaurant where if you rebel against the master, the bill mounts like it's some taxi meter.

Ono: Of course it's not. I'd be happy if you just ate normally. The restaurant exists thanks to our customers. I say these things boldly because I have nothing to lose. In March 1951, I came to Tokyo from the countryside with only one piece of luggage on me. I say luggage, but I'm talking about a long time ago, so it was made out of paper and was flimsy. That was all I owned. I was strong since that was all I could lose. I wasn't scared of getting into a fight with anyone.

Satomi: What I discovered from getting to know you for over five years to make this book is that a sushi craftsman at a good sushi restaurant is putting up a serious fight every day. It's not like customers ought to bow to them, but guests should know a certain level of manners.

Ono: I'm glad to hear that.

Satomi: What kind of customer inspires a sushi craftsman to say, "I want to make a good nigiri for this guest?"

Ono: We make nigiri right away after taking an order. So we advise you to eat it right after we make it without letting it sit there. Having it soon is the most delicious way. Nigiri doesn't get better by leaving it alone and yapping away. I can't think of anything else. I often say, "A tempura restaurant, a sushi restaurant, and a train are better when they are fast." If you're too slow, then I close the door and start the train.

Satomi: Lately, there are people who are so picky about the order of nigiri they eat. It's always prescribed in a nigiri guide.

Ono: It doesn't matter what you start or finish with. Most customers start with whatever they want to eat. If they say, "*Omakase*" (chef's choice), then I make nigiri so that the greasy items aren't back to back—I insert plain ones in the middle. But if it's à la carte, then they should order whatever they like. As I mentioned before, nigiri is for the people.

Satomi: No, no, it's no longer for the people.

Ono: Yes, it's true that it's gotten so expensive. If a customer has *omakase* until he or she is full, it costs at least 25,000 yen per person. That's not cheap. You can enjoy even *kaiseki ryori* (a traditional multi-course Japanese dinner) for 15,000 yen. But there is nothing I can do because it's about the *neta*.

Satomi: From the profit point of view, sushi restaurants that are more for the masses must make more money. The customer turnover rate is faster, and they also deliver.

Ono: Yes. Only the mass-oriented places are expanding, while the high-end ones keep shrinking.

Good sushi restaurants discipline customers

Satomi: You discussed "not making nigiri with *tai* (sea bream)" one day. Because *tai* that comes to Tsukiji doesn't measure up to *tai* from Akashi at all. However, the transportation system has developed nowadays, so if you wanted to obtain them, you could. Even from Akashi.

Ono: Yes, that's true. But I wonder if they'll send the *tai* that I'm thinking of.

Satomi: Because you can't see it for yourself?

Ono: Right, right. In which case, it's better for me to see the *hirame* (flounder) in the wintertime and the *karei* (flatfish) in the summertime with my own eyes. Plus, it's definitely not true that *hirame* from Aomori or *mako garei* (marbled sole) from Joban doesn't even compare with *tai* from Akashi.

Satomi: As a nigiri-*dane*.

Ono: Yes. For a Kansai-style *kappo* (high-end traditional restaurant), it's best to cook with seafood from the Kyoto-Osaka area, so they need *tai* from Akashi. They slice *sashimi* (raw fish). Use it for broth. Make *kabutoyaki* (grilled head). For that style of cuisine, they need *tai* from over there, but sushi restaurants that make nigiri with whitefish don't have to limit themselves to *tai* from Akashi. Especially at the Tsukiji market, they exchange fish for you if there was some error. Meanwhile, if it's shipped, I can't return it saying, "What the heck, this is no good," and I have to somehow use it. If I can't make nigiri with it, I'll have to eat it all myself.

Satomi: Ha ha ha. That would be awful.

Ono: From the end of the year to New Year's, amber-colored *hirame* from Aomori tastes really delicious if you kill it in the morning and make nigiri with it in the evening. It's far more delicious than *tai*. There is no reason to be fixated on *tai*.

Satomi: Jiro, you were born in 1925. To what age do you plan on making nigiri?

Ono: I'd like to retire soon.

Satomi: Your regulars won't let you.

Ono: That's the problem. An old face who's a doctor flatters me, saying, "You'll be all right for another couple of years," and I start to believe him.

Satomi: Well, it's common in their world, isn't it? Have your son who's working at your restaurant succeed you, and set up "the director's visiting days" like big hospitals do.

Ono: Like he comes in on Mondays, Wednesdays, and Fridays.

Satomi: At a high-end traditional place or a *unagi* (eel) restaurant, you can't see the kitchen, so it may not matter as much if the son took over. But for a business like a sushi restaurant, which exposes where a chef stands at the counter...

Ono: Yes, that's the problem.

Satomi: They often say, "A sushi lover eats the pops of the sushi restaurant." That's to say, as a sushi restaurant becomes high-end, the level of *tane*...

Ono: ...doesn't change. There are a set of good brokers at Tsukiji. And all good sushi chefs stock from them.

Satomi: So there is no chance that the best-quality *hon maguro* (bluefin tuna) goes to only one sushi restaurant.

Ono: That's correct.

Satomi: In other words, if I may exaggerate, the personality, aesthetics, and philosophy of the sushi restaurant master is expressed in *tane* that require a lot of prepping, like *kohada* (gizzard shad), *anago* (conger eel), and *kanpyo* (dried gourd). That's what decides whether someone becomes a regular. A sushi restaurant is like a membership club of people who fall in love with a master and congregate. That relationship also justifies charging off-putting customers high prices.

Ono: Yeah, I feel that half of our guests come to eat the master. For instance, if I hire a new, able hand who makes the same nigiri that I do, our guests might still think, "The fellow isn't all that." The longer they've been coming to my place, twenty, thirty years, the more likely they are to say, "When it comes to skill, Jiro beats him hands down."

Satomi: The pops changing is serious stuff for them.

Ono: Guests who make reservations come to eat the master along with the nigiri, so I can't help but feel, "It'd be rude to have Yoshi (elder son Yoshikazu), who's standing next to me at the counter, make the nigiri. As long as I can, I should make it." So while my hands still serve me, I make nigiri for this guest, and for that guest, and I end up hustling around all the time. Faced with a customer who believes that if he goes to *Jiro*, the pops will make him nigiri, I'd feel bad only saying "*irasshaimase*" (welcome) and "*maido arigato gozaimasu*" (thank you once again) at the cash register.

Satomi: It must be hard for the second generation. It would be different if their father had been irresponsible, but they need to surpass you and push themselves to soar higher and higher.

Master chefs of the Sukiyabashi Jiro franchise surround Ono and hold a social gathering once a year.

From front left: Takeshi Hiraoka (Saginomiya location), Jiro Ono, Susumu Kawabata (Nihonbashi Takashimaya location).

From back left: Nobuo Ikuma (Hamamatsu location), Daisaburo Sato (Toyosu location), Yukio Yoshiura (formerly Narawashino location), Hachiro Mizutani (Yokohama location).

Sukiyabashi Jiro staff.

From left, Yoshiko Kawabata, elder son Yoshikazu Ono, Jiro Ono, younger son Takashi Ono, Harutaka Takahashi.

Including the other staff, such as a cleaner and the dishwasher, there are eight people.

Ono: That's the issue. Where I feel I made a mistake is that I let my two sons enter the same profession. If it were a completely different path, then a child just has to start from the beginning. It's just "Ready, go," from the first step. But because we are in the same profession, it doesn't work in that "Ready, go" way.

Satomi: You're their father and their master. It's like Futagoyama *Oyakata* and the Waka-Taka brothers (famous sumo wrestler father and sons).

Ono: This is why when they're at the restaurant, my two sons are on edge. When we go home, we're just father and son, but at the restaurant they are so intimidated that they avoid me. But in the end, this is good for our customers. We won't be doing any business if the guests aren't satisfied with my sons' nigiri. I think

263

so, and that's why I don't spoil them even if they're my own. Rather, I tend to scold them more than the other young guys.

Satomi: But I think they're lucky that their starting point is not zero.

Ono: I think so too. Even after I retire, they don't have to start from zero. We have a fair number of regulars, and both my elder and my younger (Takashi) are thirtysomethings who've been training for a while. From that perspective, it's a plus, but it would have been so much easier on me if they were in different professions.

If that were the case, I'd already have retired by now. Having ceded the restaurant to some skillful, good-natured apprentice, I'd be getting paid as an adviser. Because if we closed, you wouldn't be able to lease this location anymore. And on "the director's visiting days," Monday, Wednesday, and Friday nights, I'd make a little nigiri.

Satomi: It'll be crowded on Monday, Wednesday, and Friday.

Ono: On those days, I, the medical director, will tell our guests, "Okay, you— sit there." Because I was told more than once, "Jiro's restaurant is rude. They even tell you where to sit."

Satomi: There was a time like that.

Ono: It's just that my intentions didn't get across to people.

Satomi: By the way, good sushi restaurants discipline customers. Guests at Sukiyabashi Jiro stand up to leave at 8:20, ten minutes before closing, without being told.

Ono: Come to think of it, I've never once asked a customer to stay a while ever since opening.

Satomi: Someone who doesn't know what's what might think, "What an outrageous restaurant," but that's the beauty of a sushi place that's essentially functioning on a membership basis. There's mutual respect. Because at *Jiro*, the trip to Tsukiji is made especially early in the morning.

Ono: Guests who leave early are my gods and buddhas.

Afterword to the Japanese Paperback Edition (2001)

Sukiyabashi Jiro: Making Sushi of the Season, which was published in October 1997, received unexpected support. This unconventional book about pure *Edomae*-style nigiri and natural seafood, filled with very detailed color photography, is still found in the popular titles section thanks to Jiro Ono's considerable gifts as a conversationalist as well as the devotion of the photographer, Yohei Maruyama. I was fortunate to be able to collaborate with two gentlemen of unparalleled talent.

When it came to publishing in paperback, we tried not to decrease the number of photographs, because seeing is believing [this English edition retains all of them, too].

Having read the book, if you feel like you want to try Ono's nigiri, then call and make a reservation. The master, who takes great pains on a daily basis to try to make everything taste better, awaits customers ready to face him full-on. But it's better not to expect lip service at a sushi restaurant. More often than not, the craftsman who presents the ultimate in taste uses his two hands to trap friendliness in vinegared rice, rather than in pointless words.

Now that it's made it into Bunshun Bunko [the Bungeishunju mass-market paperback line], I think it's the gods' dispensation to introduce a peerless nigiri craftsman to the world. Ono, who will be celebrating his seventy-seventh birthday in October 2001, is still in high spirits.

Note that we unfortunately had to reduce the saliva-inducing actual-size photo of *hon maguro* (bluefin tuna) that appeared as a gatefold in the original book [restored in this English edition].

—Satomi

،izuoka Prefecture, has dedicated his life to the way of the kitchen knife ever
nine years old, when he became an apprentice at an inn serving traditional
،o make it as a sushi chef, he headed to Tokyo at the age of twenty-six. The rest
to a bad burn he suffered on his right hand when he was little, he's known as "the
،ıigiri maestro."

،etagaya, Tokyo, the late **Shinzo Satomi** started a ramen shop when he was in high school
،ve up after only half a year. Despite detours—a university education in eighteenth-century
،ch literature and classical economics, and life as a "salaryman"—his culinary interests never
ated. His *Best Of* series on ramen, donburi, etc., won him renown as the proponent of an un-
،pretentious *gourmandise*.

Sushi Chef
Sukiyabashi Jiro

Production: Risa Cho

SUKIYABASHI JIRO SHUN WO NIGIRU by SATOMI Shinzo
Copyright ©1997 by NAITO Shizue
All rights reserved.

Original Japanese edition published by Bungeishunju Ltd., Japan
English translation rights reserved by Vertical, Inc., U.S.A.,
under the license granted by NAITO Shizue, Japan
arranged with Bungeishunju Ltd., Japan

Published by Vertical, Inc., New York, 2016

ISBN: 978-1-942993-27-8

Manufactured in Japan

First Edition

Second Printing

Vertical, Inc.
451 Park Avenue South, 7th Floor
New York, NY 10016
www.vertical-inc.com